Democracy and Revolutionary Politics

THEORY FOR GLOBAL AGE

Series Editors: Gurminder K. Bhambra and Robin Cohen

Editorial Board: Michael Burawoy (University of California Berkeley, USA), Neera Chandoke (University of Delhi, India), Robin Cohen (University of Oxford, UK), Peo Hansen (Linköping University, Sweden), John Holmwood (University of Nottingham, UK), Walter Mignolo (Duke University, USA), Emma Porio (Ateneo de Manila University, Philippines), Boaventura de Sousa Santos (University of Coimbra, Portugal).

Globalization is widely viewed as a current condition of the world, but there is little engagement with how this changes the way we understand it. The Theory for a Global Age series addresses the impact of globalization on the social sciences and humanities. Each title will focus on a particular theoretical issue or topic of empirical controversy and debate, addressing theory in a more global and interconnected manner. With contributions from scholars across the globe, the series will explore different perspectives to examine globalization from a global viewpoint. True to its global character, the Theory for a Global Age Series will be available for online access worldwide via Creative Commons licensing, aiming to stimulate wide debate within academia and beyond.

Each book in the series focuses on a particular theoretical issue or topic of empirical controversy and debate, addressing theory in a more comprehensive and interconnected manner in the process. With books commissioned from scholars from across the globe, the series explores understandings of the global – and global understandings – from diverse viewpoints. The series will be available in print, in eBook format and free online, through a Creative Commons licence, aiming to encourage academic engagement on a broad geographical scale and to further the reach of the debates and dialogues that the series develops.

Democracy and Revolutionary Politics

Neera Chandhoke

Bloomsbury Academic
An imprint of Bloomsbury Publishing Plc

B L O O M S B U R Y
LONDON · NEW DELHI · NEW YORK · SYDNEY

Bloomsbury Academic
An imprint of Bloomsbury Publishing Plc

50 Bedford Square
London
WC1B 3DP
UK

1385 Broadway
New York
NY 10018
USA

www.bloomsbury.com

**BLOOMSBURY and the Diana logo are trademarks of Bloomsbury
Publishing Plc**

First published 2015

British Library Cataloguing-in-Publication Data
A catalogue record for this book is available from the British Library.

ISBN: HB: 978-1-4742-2400-0
PB: 978-1-4742-2401-7
ePDF: 978-1-4742-2402-4
ePub: 978-1-4742-2403-1

Library of Congress Cataloging-in-Publication Data
A catalog record for this book is available from the Library of Congress.

Series: Theory for a Global Age

Typeset by Integra Software Services Pvt. Ltd

Contents

Series Foreword

Civil society was a key political concept at the close of the twentieth century associated, as it was, with social movements in Eastern Europe that heralded the end of the Soviet Union and the bipolar world that the 'cold war' had sustained. The twenty-first century, in turn, began with similar social movements, in other parts of the world, against monarchical regimes and authoritarian polities. From Nepal to Tunisia to Libya, people organized collectively and consistently for civil and political liberties and for democracy in various forms. While the relationship between civil society and democracy has long been charted, that between violent protest – or political violence – and democracy, less so. And yet, many of these collective mobilizations were also violent and not just contingently so.

In her important book *Democracy and Revolutionary Politics*, Neera Chandhoke argues for the necessity of examining the idea of violence, and the specificities of political or revolutionary violence, in the context of classical concerns with the main subjects of political theory – justice and the state. Since Weber, the latter has been directly associated with a claim to legitimacy for a monopoly over violence within a given territory, with democratic sovereignty the currently accepted basis of that claim to legitimacy. Given the impact of violence and, in particular, revolutionary violence, upon the shaping of democratic states, Chandhoke argues, it is not possible simply to dismiss non-state violence, or to look for single-issue explanations – justifications or condemnations – that either place it outside the dynamics of democratic politics or as hostile to it. Instead, the book is a meticulous working through of the complexities and ambiguities of political violence and an intimate examination of its relation to theoretical and actual contradictions of democratic politics.

This work of theory is undertaken through an examination of the armed struggle waged by Maoists in democratic India and asks two interrelated questions: can revolutionary violence be justified in democratic contexts and in what circumstances can it be justified? Even if it can be justified, Chandhoke continues, is it a prudent way of doing politics in democracies? This ambiguity forms the central point of the argument. As Chandhoke perceptively notes, what is at issue here is the necessity, always, of being able to claim justice from the state, even if – and perhaps especially if – that state understands itself as democratic. While much of the book addresses violence through an empirical lens focused on the politics of the Maoists, the conclusion addresses the political thought of one of the most renowned proponents of non-violence, Mohandas Karamchand Gandhi.

The book is a superb illustration of one of the key aims of the Theory for a Global Age series, namely, of seeking to understand what 'theory' might look like if we started from places other than Europe and from persons other than European thinkers. The focus on an episode from the history of the global South is illuminating about that episode, but actually does much more as well. It provides an excellent exposition of the possibilities of how the conceptual and political debates on violence, especially political violence, can be broadened and enriched by taking a global perspective.

Gurminder K. Bhambra

Acknowledgements

I began work on this project when I joined Rainer Forst's research programme *Justitia Amplificata*, Goethe University, Frankfurt, as senior fellow (2012–2013). I wish to express my profound gratitude to Rainer for his support and friendship. During the period of the fellowship, I stayed at *Forschungskolleg Humanwissenschaften* at Bad Homburg. The institute provided ideal surroundings for sustained work, as well as relaxation amidst the company of other scholars. Thanks to Ingrid, Beate and Andreas for making my stay such a pleasant one. I recollect our treks in more than ankle-deep snow in the middle of the German winter, to visit a restaurant or a micro-brewery, with great nostalgia.

Back in Delhi, I began to write up the work as National Fellow, Indian Council of Social Science Research, New Delhi (2013–2015). Thanks to Professor Sukhdeo Thorat, the chairman of the ICSSR, Professor Ramesh Dadich, member-secretary, and Dr Sanchita Dutta, for their co-operation and help. I was affiliated to the Centre for Contemporary Studies, Nehru Memorial Museum and Library, Teen Murti House, New Delhi, during the period of the fellowship. As always, it is a pleasure to work in the magnificent library of the NMML, stroll through sylvan surroundings and participate in seminar programmes. My gratitude to Professor Mahesh Rangarajan and Dr Balakrishnan. May NMML flourish even more under the able guidance of Mahesh.

Preliminary presentations on the theme of revolutionary violence were made at the political theory seminar organized by Stephan Gosepath at Free University Berlin, Rainer's political theory colloquium at Goethe Frankfurt, Centre for Ethics and Global Politics at LUISS Rome and the conference on Maoism organized by Ajay Gudavarthy at Jawaharlal Nehru University in Delhi. Some very sharp and insightful questions enabled me to reflect on the intricate problems that stalk the issue of revolutionary violence. I want to thank Nancy Fraser, a co-fellow at *Justitia*, for encouraging me to think in terms of 'revolutionary' rather than the vocabulary of bland 'political' violence. My thanks to Sebastiano Maffetone and Valentina Gentile at LUISS for many kindnesses.

As academic editor-in-charge of the 'Theory for a Global Age' series at Bloomsbury, UK, Gurminder Bhambra has been most encouraging. She piloted the manuscript through the pre-publication stage with exemplary efficiency. Profound thanks Gurminder. I want to express my gratitude to Caroline Wintersgill and Jyoti Basuita at Bloomsbury for all their ready and effective cooperation.

Above all I wish to thank Partho Dutta, with whom I discussed over endless tea sessions at India International Centre the possibility of writing a semi-popular book free of the rigidities of social science arguments even before I thought of the theme. He read through the entire manuscript, as did Achin Vanaik. Thanks guys. Achin and I continue to disagree over the contribution of Che Guevara to the theory of revolutionary violence, but I am indebted to him for detailed comments. My gratitude to John Harriss for readily extending reassurance at every stage of the work. I will never tire of thanking my small and valued group of friends in Delhi who sustain me personally and professionally, Rama, Renu, Niraja, Aakash and Karan. My children continue to give me enormous strength and happiness. Finally, many thanks to the ever smiling and cooperative staff of the India International Centre Library.

Introduction

Protest politics in the twenty-first century

Civil society

The first two decades of the twenty-first century witnessed the intensification of two starkly dissimilar forms of protest across the global south. From Nepal to Libya, huge crowds, driven by a distinctly anti-authoritarian mood, assembled and agitated in public spaces to demand an end to monarchical rule, dictatorships and individualized tyrannies. The mobilization of civil societies against undemocratic governments once again, after 1989, demonstrated the competence of the political public to participate in an activity the ancient Greeks had termed politics.

Collective action bred dramatic results, at least in some countries. In 2006, in Nepal, a massive anti-monarchy movement was transmuted in the course of the struggle into a pro-democracy movement. The movement brought an end to a monarchy that had once claimed divine right to rule, motivated the Maoists to lay aside their weapons and take part in elections to a constituent assembly and catapulted the transition of the Nepali people from subject to citizen. Over two years, 2007 and 2008, a pro-democracy movement, led by lawyers, shook up the then military-ruled Pakistan. The movement forced the military government under General Parvez Musharraf to its knees, and heralded yet again the return of democratic politics to the country.

The most fervent assertion of civil society occurred in a region that had been written off by many scholars as destined for authoritarian rule, the Arab world. A series of anti-government protests, uprisings and rebellions in early 2011 inaugurated what came to be known as the 'Arab Spring' that spread from Tunisia to Egypt, to Syria. The term 'Arab

Spring' is hotly contested, but roughly it captures the phenomenon of a political awakening, and vocal articulation of discontent. Relatively peaceful crowds, passionately pursuing liberty, fundamental rights, constitutional and accountable government and above all dignity occupied and agitated in public spaces. Even as the initial uprising in Tunisia exerted a domino effect in the rest of the region, the development evoked reminiscences of 'Velvet Revolutions' in East Europe in 1989 that heralded the demise of Stalinist states and initiated electoral democracy and market economies. Since 1989, some very powerful states have collapsed like the proverbial house of cards before civil societies single-mindedly pursuing the agenda of democracy.

Certainly, there is more to civil society than just mobilization against tyrannical regimes. The concept abstracts from, describes and conceptualizes particular sorts of politics, such as civic activism and collective action. It is normative in so far as it specifies that associational life in a metaphorical space between the household, the market and the state is valuable. Associational life neutralizes the individualism, the atomism and the anomie that modernity brings in its wake. Social associations enable pursuit of multiple projects, and thereby engender solidarity. The projects themselves range from developing popular consciousness about climate change, to discussing and dissecting popular culture, to supporting needy children, to organizing neighbourhood activities, to monitoring the state. Above all, the concept recognizes that even democratic states are likely to be imperfect. Democracy is a project that has to be realized through sustained engagement with holders of power. Citizen activism, public vigilance, informed public opinion, a free media and a multiplicity of social associations are necessary preconditions for this task.[1]

But it was the minimal avatar of civil society, that of mobilization against authoritarian regimes that denied, as dictatorships are wont to do, civil and political liberties to the people, which moved thousands of people across the globe to stand up and speak back to a history not of their making. The wheel had turned full circle. In 1971, Solidarity in Poland had reinvented the concept of civil society. This reinvented concept spread to other parts of eastern and central Europe. It swept to Brazil where urban professional classes, youth and women's movements, trade unions and social associations took on the military regime, and to other parts of South America. And the concept enthused individuals and groups in South Asia and the Arab world to demand what is their rightful due.

A reinvented civil society that drew upon De Tocqueville more than Hegel or Gramsci gave to the world a new vocabulary: of participation, of civic and associational life, of the right of citizens to hold governments responsible and of human rights. The vocabulary contributed a great deal to the spread of the *idea* of democracy even if the institutionalization of democracy in large parts of the world remains an incomplete venture, a dream but partly realized. The language of civil society also gave to inhabitants of non-democracies and imperfect democracies hopes that the future would bring them rights and dignity, that democracy would be realized and that the capacity of ordinary human beings to realize themselves through collective action and social movements would be recognized and valued.

Political violence

This is not, however, the end of the story of people's resistance to excessive and arbitrary power wielded by state elites. The task of civil society is to monitor and protest against elite capture of institutions and of resources, and against unwarranted state control over lives. That is why civil society is an essential precondition of democracy. But in country after country, civil society lost momentum in the face of inflexible states, or descended into proactive and/or reactive violence as in Egypt. At the very time that the phrase 'civil society' came onto the political tongues of newspaper readers, the social media, and television audiences, we also witnessed an explosion of politics in the mode of violence, in other words political violence.

Protest and resistance in the mode of violence is, of course, not new to human kind. The twentieth century can rightly be called the 'age of violence', given the immense destruction wrought by two world wars, numerous proxy wars, colonial despotism, anti-colonial guerrilla struggles and civil wars in the post-colony. Colonial rulers left countries they had plundered in states of devastation and were quickly replaced by a new, appropriative ruling class in the post-colony.

The persistence of injustice, exploitation, oppression and marginalization in the post-colony bred expected results in the form of violent resistance. Anti-colonial struggles subsided after fulfilling the objective of winning independence. The political space they vacated was occupied by new sorts of armed struggle within the post-colony, over the right of a particular ethnic group to rule, for control of resources, for takeover of state power or for a state of one's own. Formal colonialism came to an end, but colonialism was recast as economic imperialism that intensified deprivation and misery for the poor in the global south and generated multiple mutinies. An impoverished peasantry took to arms against institutionalized injustice within the post-colony; and private armies of aspirant elites sought to imprint the body politic with partisan and avaricious agendas.

The first two decades of the twenty-first century proved no exception to this trend of violent politics. Some non-state groups continue to use immense violence to assert claims to state power, others use violence to oppose the monopoly of power by political elites and yet other groups use violence to make a statement, to assert the power of the group and to create a generalized atmosphere of fear and trepidation. The last is best captured in the phrase 'global terrorism', which with a degree of impunity destroys lives and infrastructure at will.

Above all, post-colonies experienced unprecedented violence because some or the other group within the country staked a claim for a state of its own. The laws of secession or attempted secessions in the post-colonial world are frankly the laws of war – laws of the jungle. The reason why secessions are so messy in the post-colonial world, compared to, for example, the wished-for secessions in Scotland and Catalonia from parent countries, is fairly obvious. For countries that wrested independence from colonial powers in the second half of the twentieth century, secession signifies a dramatic failure, a failure to consolidate the territory of the nation state.

The nation state is highly overrated, and in our part of the world, South Asia, it appears as one of the major mistakes of history. Even so, the global community continues to hold fast to the belief that the only state worth its name is a nation state and continues to believe that the 'nation' should form an essential prefix to the state, as in the axiom the 'nation-state'. In the global order, states that cannot hold their territory together are castigated as failed states, as crisis states and as fragile states, by western governments, donors, rating agencies and western academics for whom research on 'failed states' has become a profitable industry. The terminology produces anxiety, political knees quake and spines of ruling elite quiver. For any one of these dubious titles casts a particularly dark shadow on state capacity. The tale of terrible vengeance wreaked on insurgency by states could have been foretold.

States in the global south have responded by accelerating 'nation-building' through coercive means. There are a great many tragedies waiting to happen in, for example South Asia, simply because state making has not been preceded by 'nation making' as was the case in Italy and France. Post-colonial states simply cannot come to terms with loss of territory. They resort to every means available: torture, encounter deaths, firing on peaceful protests, imprisonment at will, draconian legislation, displacement and suspension of civil and political liberties, to repress secession.

The dramatic expansion in the number of groups demanding a state of one's own dates to the collapse of actually existing socialist societies at the turn of the 1990s. This inaugurated an era of violent ethno-nationalist movements, especially in the region of the Balkans and the Caucasus. The consequences of the upsurge were, somewhat, serious. Countries dissolved, federal systems melted away and a number of new states emerged out of the debris of old ones often through processes of armed struggle, ethnic cleansing and genocide. Not surprisingly, a new lease of life was infused into hitherto dormant separatist movements. Among some examples of these movements are the Kashmiri's, the Naga's and the Bodo's in India; the Chechens in Russia; separatist movements in Azerbaijan (Nagorno-Karabach) and Moldova (Trans-Dniester); Baluchistan in Pakistan; West Papua in Indonesia; the Oromos and the Somalis in Ethiopia; the Kurds in Turkey; till May 2009 the Tamils in Sri Lanka; South Ossetia and Abkhazia in Georgia; and parts of the Ukraine.

Political violence in the global south

In some cases, secessionist movements have proved victorious. But wresting a state of one's own out of unwilling hands has hardly managed to resolve problems of ethnic, religious or linguistic minorities.[2] Consider Georgia and Ukraine that gained independence with the meltdown of the former superpower, the USSR. Both these countries have been wracked by separatist violence that has proved successful in some regions – notably Abkhazia and South Ossetia. Crimea became independent vide a referendum held in the shadow of an army massed at the border. Separatism has succeeded but will the formation of yet another state, or, as in the case of Crimea, integration into another state unscramble the basic problems that bedevilled earlier avatars of state formation? Recollect that in South Sudan, violence exploded between the two main ethnic communities almost immediately after it achieved independence in July 2011.

Afghanistan since 2013 has entered a new phase of civil war, marked by escalating violence between insurgents and the Afghan National Security Forces. The retreat of international security forces and the rapid decline in the capacity of the Afghan government to control the situation have led to generalized terrorism that affects neighbouring countries. Even as the insurgents assemble bigger formation for assaults,[3] Afghanistan provides but one case of what Praveen Swami calls 'epic wars unleashed by Mr Bush in the wake of 9/11'. Islamist armies more powerful than before 'have swept aside Iraq's military in Mosul, Tikrit, and Bayji; in Syria, too, they control large swathes of territory. Yemen has all but disintegrated. Pakistan is in apparently terminal meltdown. Iran and Saudi Arabia, the two largest regional powers, have been eyeing each other warily – each wondering when the ethnic-religious fires raging across the region will ignite a full-blown war between them'.[4] Other horrifying cases of political violence continue to make for dismal newspaper reading every morning: Darfur, Central African Republic, Democratic Republic of Congo, Eastern Burma, Eastern Chad, Iraq, Syria, Somalia and Sri Lanka. These regions stand as signifiers of brutality and terror, of man's inhumanity to man.

There seems to be no end to the spiral of civil wars and political violence in the foreseeable future (I am not speaking of global terrorism for this phenomenon demands a separate argument). Private armies augment arsenals, recruit civilians and often little children to fight their wars and assault the state. States fortify their walls against offensives that mercilessly batter their ramparts. And ordinary citizens are caught in the crossfire. The consequences are disastrous: loss of livelihood and lives, displacement and banishment to refugee camps, where relocated people are vulnerable to disease, malnutrition and general ill-being.

The United Nations High Commission for Refugees reports that for the first time since the Second World War the number of people driven from their homes by conflict and crisis touched 51.2 million by the end of 2013. Syria is the hardest hit. 'We are seeing here the immense costs of not ending wars, of failing to resolve or prevent conflict', said the UNHCR chief Antonio Guterres. Without political solutions, he continued, 'alarming levels of conflict and the mass suffering that is reflected in these figures will continue'.[5] The intensification of extreme violence in Iraq and Syria by the ISIS (Islamic State of Iraq and Syria) has worsened the plight of ordinary people.

Conceptualizing political violence

Given the pervasiveness of political violence, political theorists have had to take on board the generic concept of violence, the specificities of political violence and increasingly terrorism.[6] Some of these formulations are discussed during the course of this argument. The urgency of the situation gives us enough reason to try to explore the concept of political violence and sort out categories of this genre of politics. First, political violence significantly impacts the classical concerns of the subject of political theory: the indispensability of an impartial and fair state, sanctity of human rights, civility, pluralism, toleration, secularism and above all injustice and justice. Second, political violence impacts the context in which we live and work. The subject cannot be relegated to a space outside the ambit of concern of political theorists.

But how do political theorists go about conceptualizing political violence? What conceptual tools do we have to theorize acts that cause immense harm and leave ineradicable scars on the body politic? There are conceivably two ways in which we can do so. First, we can believe that the origins of political violence, which aims to take over state power, control resources or pursue ethnic vengeance and/or the righting of historic wrongs, can be traced to that catch-all term ethnicity and ancient rivalries between groups. Or, we could say that insurgency is driven by greed for control over resources such as minerals and agro-products, and that rank acquisitiveness wins over politics of ethnic angst. According to the well-known thesis put forth by Paul Collier and Anke Hoeffler, most civil wars are driven by greed and grievance with the former dominating the latter.[7] It may well be that the ethnic fig leaf is used to camouflage rank avarice.

On the other hand, and this is the second route to conceptualizing political violence, we recognize that such neat explanations serve to push issues of justice and injustice, of exploitation and resistance, of justifiability and of contradictions in the practice of armed non-state actors, under the metaphorical carpet. This does not help anyone to take a principled stand on the issue of political violence, unless we happen to be either uncritical ideologues or fervent opponents of this form of politics. As uncritical ideologues, we could affirm with some ease that political violence is needed because the world is violent. And as fervent opponents, we would say that violence by non-state actors is a pox on our earth and should be exterminated by the use of every means possible.

But certain sorts of political violence I suggest in this work, particularly revolutionary violence, do not and cannot permit of single-point explanatory agendas or solutions, impassioned affirmation or fanatical disapproval. All political concepts are complex and contradictory, but political violence is more complex, more contradictory and definitely untidier than most concepts. As we shall see in the course of this argument, it is possible to support as well as reject this form of politics at the same time. We can understand why groups have reached for the nearest gun, and yet believe that political violence is a bad or rather an unwise way of doing politics in a democracy.

If we recognize the ambivalences of political violence, and if we understand that the specificities of political violence can only be comprehended and justified contextually, as the argument in this work holds, our agenda shifts. Abjuring outright affirmations or dismissals, we begin to ask a different set of questions. For instance, are armed insurgents justified in using violence to press their demands regardless of whether or not they will win the struggle? What are the circumstances in which they have resorted to violence? What are the contradictions in this particular avatar of politics? What precisely does this sort of politics do for ordinary people: does it enable them to recover 'voice', realize the enormity of injustice heaped upon them and fight for justice? Or, does political violence reduce people to an audience of a political theatre of the absurd, where every protagonist, as in Greek tragedies, either commits suicide or is killed? What is the concept of violence about, in any case?

The issue that lies at the heart of violence should be clear by now. For critical political theorists, discussions about political violence are ultimately about the kind of state that does or does not provide justice to its people *even* if it is democratic. This we have to take into account. We have to recognize that justice and democracy may not be conceptual siblings and that sometimes violence has to be used to seize justice from states. If this is not of interest for political theory, what is? Political theorists have to ask why people rebel in a democracy that recognizes the value of dissent. Finally, discussions about violence in political theory are eventually about what violent politics contribute to the lives of those very people this avatar of the political speaks for. There is, in other words, paramount need to think through the concept of political violence, its nuances, its inconsistencies and its complexities.

For this reason, I approach the theme of political or more specifically revolutionary violence from the vantage point of critical political theory. (I use in the rest of the work the terms 'revolutionary and political violence', and 'revolutionary violence' and 'revolutionary politics' interchangeably because revolutionary violence, arguably, represents an extreme form of the political.)

The significance of empirical referrals

But, then, political theory has to address empirical contexts and concrete problems. 'The task of political theory', John Dunn reminds us, 'is to diagnose practical predicaments and to show us how best to confront them'.[8] Arguably, political theory as critical activity is geared to addressing and reflecting on intractable political problems and dilemmas of the human condition. Therefore, practitioners of the craft cannot afford to live and work in rarified spaces shorn of the complications of actually existing social, economic and political worlds. If the task of political theorists is to figure out what this form of politics we call political violence is about, and why it has erupted onto the political landscape, then our theories cannot ignore empirical facts that constitute a referral for theories in the first place.

In any case, in a world that is inscribed with inflexible political predicaments can theorists resort only to formal propositions and hypothetical examples to illustrate the finer points of their formulations? Does he or she have any other option except to philosophically reflect on and try and sort out the ambivalences, the uncertainties and the contingent nature of the political world?

Of course, we may not be able to come up with neat theories if we try and negotiate situations and circumstances that are far from neat. Coppieters has made an important point in the context of secession. For him, any approach that

> avoids tackling the innumerable difficulties inherent in the precise description and analysis of a concrete case of secession, does have clear advantages. It makes it possible to clarify the moral debate on secession when discussing the hierarchical order of various legal and philosophical principles and arguments within a systematic framework... [Yet] philosophical reflection on the guiding principles applicable in a normative analysis of the legitimacy of secession cannot be made in a way that is entirely abstracted from practical experience.[9]

The danger is of course that theories that address empirical situations and facts become much more hesitant and shorn of certainties, convictions and neatness. But this might be an advantage, because seldom do political dilemmas and uncertainties lend themselves to absolutely clear and unreservedly decisive analysis, conclusions and resolutions. It is just as well that we recognize this particular aspect of politics that we seek to understand, theorize and prescribe for.

The significance of political theory

The task of political theory is to critically engage with political practices and quandaries; therefore, theorists need an empirical referent point.

At the same time, we should be careful not to lapse into empiricism. 'Whereas', suggests Daniel McDermott, 'social scientists determine the empirical facts of human behaviour and institutions, political philosophers aim to determine what ought to be done in light of that information. How should states be organized? What kinds of projects should they pursue? Are there some actions that are impermissible?' No set of empirical facts can answer these questions. Empirical facts are important, but without 'the normative element that is the political philosopher's concern, nothing would follow about which form of government ought to be implemented'.[10]

Accordingly, this study attempts to explore the concept of violence from the vantage point of critical political theory, which in turn addresses the armed struggle waged by Maoists in India. India provides an interesting referral for the theme. Political theorists generally agree that political violence has no room in a democracy, which gives voice to its citizens. India is unquestionably a democracy. Yet all sorts of violence bedevil political life in democratic India as in other countries, from secession, to communal and caste riots, to revolutionary violence. We have to make sense of this paradox.

Arguably, two key questions constitute the core of a political theory of revolutionary violence. First, can we justify revolutionary violence in democratic contexts? In what circumstances can we justify political/revolutionary violence? The problem is elaborated in Chapter 1 and negotiated in Chapter 4. Political violence can be justified, I argue in Chapter 4, in a very specific set of circumstances – that of overlapping forms of injustice that betray the basic presuppositions of democracy. The underlying theme of this work is the relationship between democracy and revolutionary violence.

Second, even if we can justify revolutionary violence with reference to some criterion, is this a prudent way of doing politics in a democracy? Revolutionary violence claims to speak in the name of and for the most marginalized in society, but what exactly does this form of politics do for its constituency? Does it enable voice? Before we negotiate these questions, there is need, I argue in Chapter 2, to sort out the many meanings ascribed to violence. In Chapter 3, I outline a brief biography of revolutionary violence in India. And in the conclusion, I revisit a period of Indian history to discover what Gandhi had to say about revolutionary violence in the country. Though Gandhi is known more for his strong belief in non-violence, he actually had carefully thought through extremist violence that wracked India at the turn of the twentieth century. Many of his insights enable us to comprehend the nature of revolutionary violence.

Objectives of the argument

Objective I: A perspective from the global south

Whereas the Maoist problem constitutes the empirical linchpin of the argument, this is not another book on Maoism. This study is distinctive, I hope, not because it gathers, documents and analyses knowledge about the Maoist armed struggle, not because it tries to explain the whys or the whereof of the political crisis and not because it rehearses explanatory theories already on board, but because it tries to do something else with the knowledge already gleaned, and with theories already constructed. This 'something else' consists of reflecting on the nature of, justifications for and the contradictions in revolutionary violence.

The argument might be able to contribute to the conceptual and the political debate on violence from the perspective of the global south. Where else would a voice on revolutionary violence come from? The global south is more than familiar with this avatar of politics. In the past, Maoist violence had flared up in predominantly agrarian countries in the form of an anti-colonial liberation war. Armed anti-imperialist struggles had swept China, Vietnam, Mozambique, Angola, Guinea-Bissau and Algeria. In the post-colonial period, revolutionary violence shattered the complacencies of Indian democracy and challenged the legitimacy of the state in the name of the most deprived, the most discriminated against and the voiceless.

I attempt to contribute to the debate on violence from this particular spatial and experiential vantage point.

Objective II: Towards a dialogue on political violence

I do not seek to glean policy prescriptions for the Indian state, or indeed for the revolutionaries from this study, because I believe that the task of scholarship is to keep a dialogue going not only in the havens of political theory, such as journals and seminars, but also in public spaces. In any case, no theorist, or expert, or activist can ever declare that he or she has said the final word on an issue, that nothing more needs to be said and that 'this' or 'that' requires to be done. For knowledge is necessarily imperfect, and inescapably partial. Two political philosophers living in different centuries and in different spaces were to tell us precisely this. The first of these was the Athenian philosopher Socrates (469BC–399BC).

In Plato's *Apology*, Socrates defends his case before an Athenian jury thus. The late Chaerephon who was a friend of mine, he said, went to Delphi and asked the oracle to tell him who the wisest man of Athens was. The Pythian prophetess answered that there was no man wiser than Socrates. Confessing that he was bewildered by this answer, because 'I know that I have no wisdom, small or great', Socrates set out on a voyage of discovery. He intended to find out who in Athens was wiser than him. It is only then that he could go to the God and refute the statement. I, said Socrates, spoke to politicians, poets and artisans, all of whom had a reputation for wisdom. And I came away time after time with the conviction that 'I am better off than he is – for he knows nothing, and thinks that he knows; I neither know nor think that I know'.

The truth is 'O men of Athens', stated the philosopher, 'that God only is wise; and by his answer he intends to show that the wisdom of men is worth little or nothing; he is not speaking of Socrates, he is only using my name by way of illustration, as if he said, He, O men, is the wisest, who, like Socrates, knows that his wisdom is in truth worth nothing'.[11]

In this passage, Socrates addressed one of the staple problems in philosophy: how do we know that we know. The answer is that we can never know whether we know. All that we can be certain of is that there are limits to our knowledge.

In the twentieth century, another philosopher M.K. Gandhi made roughly the same argument. For Gandhi, truth is absolute and transcendental, but human beings cannot possibly know what the absolute truth is. Gandhi cites a story in the Gospel to establish this point. A judge wants to know what the truth is, but gets no answer. The question posed by that judge, suggests Gandhi, has still not been answered. This is because truth means different things to different people. The truth espoused by King Harishchandra, who renounced everything he possessed for the sake of the truth, is not the same as the truth of Hussain, who sacrificed his life for the truth. These two truths are equally true, albeit partially so, but they may or may not be *our* truth. Gandhi, in effect, tells us that the one ultimate truth is manifested in the shape of many truths, but each of these truths is but an incomplete version of the ultimate truth. Using the metaphor of the seven blind men and the elephant, Gandhi suggests that we are as blind as the seven in the story.[12] We miss out on the wood for the trees.

The proposition that human beings can, but, partially grasp the nature of the ultimate truth holds interesting implications. First, the nature of Gandhi's truth enjoins human beings to discover the truth along with others in and through dialogical interaction, and through a shared search for the Holy Grail. We will never reach the site of the Holy Grail, but that is not important, what is important is the journey transforms our understanding. Second, if persons have the capacity to know the truth, but not the entire truth, then no one person or group can claim superiority over another on the ground that their truth alone is the ultimate truth, and that other truths are false or travesties of the real thing. Such beliefs – that only we know the truth – are the basic cause of violence. Not only is Gandhi's notion of toleration anchored in his theory of imperfect knowledge, this theory gives us ground to believe that the search for truth has to be a collective effort.

Gandhi would deny that inability to know the entire truth leads to moral relativism. All that he expects is that people arrive at judgements about the world they encounter in full awareness that these judgements are partial. No one can know all there is to know about any subject. Nor can they be certain that what they know is the truth and nothing but the truth. They might have to change their minds during the course of their lives as they encounter other people, other beliefs, other truths and when they become aware of other possibilities. Our truth is always subject to renegotiation. The proposal that truth is always subject to renegotiation sounds absurd but is nevertheless reflective of the state of human knowledge. All that we can do is to keep our minds open to other perspectives and other takes on an issue that we have judged, but, provisionally.

We, as a matter of course, cannot appreciate other perspectives unless we are willing to listen to other people, until we are ready to respect their views. We might find that we were wrong, misguided, confused, or all three. Such abashed recognition is as true of personal transactions as of political ones.

Take, for instance, Jane Austen's deservedly famous and popular novel *Pride and Prejudice*. The introduction tells us that this novel tells us how a man changes his manners, and a young lady changes her mind. The protagonist of the novel, Elizabeth, sets herself against the highly attractive Mr Darcy for a number of reasons. One of these reasons is that he had treated a friend of hers, Wickham, shabbily. Or so she believes. Elizabeth blushes at her own lack of judgement the moment she comes to know the other side of the story from Darcy himself. 'She grew absolutely ashamed of herself.-Of neither Darcy nor Wickham could she think, without feeling that she had been blind, partial, prejudiced, absurd.'[13] The message of this most charmingly written novel is as follows. Rather than rushing to acclaim or condemn anything, we need to think through various aspects of the issue and take care to consider other opinions and other dimensions.

The simple act of 'listening' to opposing points of view will allow us to re-examine our own beliefs. An unexamined life as Socrates had reminded us is really not worth living. Above all, there is nothing, but nothing, like dialogue to depress pretensions that we know everything there is to know. Dialogue instils modesty in our own capacities to understand, analyse, predict and resolve. We would do well to remember that in Greek mythology hubris or overweening pride and arrogance that human beings can even dare chart out paths that we and others will traverse in the future was likely to be dramatically overturned by a certain avenging goddess called Nemesis. This particular affectation falls within the provenance of the Gods; it is not for human beings to believe that they know all there is to know about the world.

Above all, engagement in dialogue is indispensable because the give and take of ideas unearths the complexities of an issue and shows us how best to approach these complexities. Politics is plural, contested and often messy, and a given political problem, say political violence, has probably more than two sides to it. To cut down on these complexities makes for bad political understanding. We cannot be sure that we know all that there is to know about a particular issue or a problem. All that we can do is to engage with others in a conversation that might tell us about other stories of a mega story. It is in this spirit that I try to unpack the narrative of revolutionary/political violence as a contribution to the general discussion on violence.

Objective III: Mapping complexities

In keeping with the reductive mood of the times, the debate on revolutionary violence in India has been deeply polarized with a majority of participants castigating Maoists. Critics argue strenuously that violence by non-state groups is immoral, destructive of society, irresponsible and unwarranted, and that groups that deal in violence are criminals or terrorists. A few observers and analysts defend Maoists as fighters for a worthwhile cause and thus defend violence as justified. Not only is the debate polarized between the 'Yays and the 'Nays', political violence is dismissed as a law and order problem, submerged in the generic concept of violence or casually labelled as structural violence. The specificities of revolutionary violence simply go missing in the process. It is the specificity of revolutionary violence that I wish to deal with in this essay.

To rephrase the first of the two questions that have already been tabled, and that form the anchor of this work: is it possible that violence by non-state actors can be prima facie justified? The addition of the term 'prima-facie' as a prefix to 'justified' holds significant implications. Arguably, violence does not lend itself to absolute and unconditional defence, the way we defend the legitimate right to protest or the right to civil disobedience in a democracy. Violence or more precisely political violence is capable of prima facie justification in very specific circumstances. What are these conditions? The exploration of this question is one objective of this work.

Inbuilt into the notion of prima facie justification is that the argument at hand can be mediated or overruled by other considerations. Let me clarify. Through reflective and critical engagement with the issue at hand, it is possible to conclude that violence by non-state actors can be justified in certain and in very specific circumstances. But, then, other problems with political violence rear their head and propel a rethink. As the second question that has been put on the high table of reflection and judgement asks: is revolutionary violence a prudent way of doing politics? Perhaps yes, perhaps no. We can know this only when we open up the concept of revolutionary/political violence, examine and learn from the history of this sort of violence and critically engage with the question of whether revolutionary violence fulfils its own presuppositions.

Paradoxes and ambivalences

Note that I am not speaking of the morality or the immorality of violence, nor do I say that violence is an absolute wrong. Of course violence is a wrong, but the deplorable conditions in which people, who revolutionaries pick up the gun for, live are also a wrong. The banishment of entire groups to regions lying outside the pale of state and public concern is equally immoral. Eschewing immorality and notions of wrong, I speak of the ambiguities that track the path of revolutionary violence. I ask whether revolutionary violence fulfils its own presuppositions.

For this reason, we cannot reduce the question whether violence is justified to either–or answers. In a world shot through with contradictions and ambiguities, we have to recognize that violence may be necessary in some cases, even if we opt for non-violence. We recognize the inevitability of violence in specified instances, even as we recognize that this mode of politics can be politically unwise and even counterproductive.

This does not make for neat theory or single-point explanations. But, then, it is impossible to make definitive judgements about ideologies and acts that use force and coercion to achieve objectives that every egalitarian democrat dreams of. Revolutionary violence, to put the point across mildly, is an ambiguous concept. Ambiguity is, nevertheless, not a bad thing, because it allows us to investigate different aspects of a question without subordinating these to a mega story. Recognition of ambiguity is not a bad thing, because it allows departure from the rigorous rules of consistency in social science arguments; rules of consistency that are unfair to inconsistent political phenomenon. And ambiguity is not a bad thing because the world of politics that we inhabit is shot through with discrepancies and irreconcilable paradoxes. An attempt to bring neatness in explanation or prescription into understandings of these practices can prove flawed, for politics of this sort does not lend itself to single-point agendas and simplistic solutions. To impose coherence upon processes that are necessarily untidy and incoherent is to prevent understanding of, well, how untidy and incoherent politics can be.

A conceptual analysis of the politics of revolutionary violence, an analysis of the context in which it has arisen, a study of the constituency which it caters to, a focus on what it stands for and what it does not stand for might well lead us to conclude along with Hamlet that there 'are more things in heaven and earth, Horatio, than are dreamt of in your philosophy'. Recollect that these immortal lines penned by Shakespeare were uttered by Hamlet to Horatio who was in a state of utter bewilderment, even paralysis, at the spectacle of Hamlet conversing with the ghost of his own father, the late king of Denmark. Like Hamlet, Horatio was a student at the University of Wittenberg where he studied classical philosophy. And classical philosophy grounded in ethics, logic and the natural sciences is hardly likely to admit that ghosts exist. But perhaps in other systems of perception and beliefs, and for those who possess the famed 'sixth sense', ghosts do exist.[14]

Likewise, political violence, which is a form of politics even if it is non-standard, admits of more than rational philosophy gives us reason to assume; that the only conclusion worth arriving at should be consistent and non-contradictory. In the final instance, we have to take sides according to judgements that are necessarily married to uncertainty, caution and prudence. Traditionally, the concept of prudence is seen as synonymous with practical wisdom, a virtue that is the hallmark of Aristotle's notion of *phronesis*. As a property of the practical intellect, prudence tells us that it is better we err on the side of caution, temperance and fortitude, instead of rashly acclaiming, condemning or dismissing violence outright.

In any case, I do not aspire to make a definitive statement on revolutionary violence, but, then, no one can pronounce a definitive judgement on anything. All arguments, even those made by intellectual giants, can be, but, contributions to an ongoing conversation. What I wish to do is to lay out some of the nuances and contradictions in the political practice of revolutionary violence. Towards that end in this work, I make a case *for* political violence, and one *against* political violence. This is, perhaps, in the best tradition of argument. After we make an argument, we turn it on its head, and look at the other side of the issue. That is, we seriously investigate both sides of an issue, and employ judgement marked by prudence to see which side is more persuasive.

Conclusion

On balance, most people seldom go beyond familiar political languages and beliefs and ask questions that run against the grain of received wisdom. The sheer ubiquity of received wisdom on a number of issues forecloses the asking of uncomfortable questions about, say, revolutionary violence. But these must be asked because they matter for democracy and for us. We are, after all, bound to other citizens by virtue of common membership of a political community. We have obligations towards them; the obligation to ensure that they are not deprived of justice that is the rightful due of every citizen. We have the duty to investigate whether they are justified in issuing a call to arms. At the same time we are also bound to interrogate political practices, especially if these political practices are cast in the garb of violence. Violence is a form of politics, and whether it is employed by the state or by non-state actors, it shapes the larger political context in which we live and work. In the next chapter, I explore the relationship between democracy and violence, focus on state violence and categorize political violence.

Democratic theorists have to take on the issue of political violence in democracies. The hope that democracies have no room for violence has been belied. Our belief that democratic deliberation is the only way to resolve problems has been shattered. In any case, a defence of non-violent politics demands that we think through violence. This is after all what Gandhi did, as we will see in the concluding chapter of this work.[15]

Democracy and Revolutionary Violence

Introduction

At first sight political violence appears to be an anomaly in democratic theory. Why should groups pick up the gun, or support those who do so, when they have the democratic right to question and renegotiate justice, in and through struggles in civil society. By contrast, the route that political violence takes is unpredictable and dangerous. It leads to harm, bears consequences that may well be unintended such as deaths of innocent bystanders, generates fear and resentment in civil society, loses out on the sympathy quotient, invites retaliation on a massive scale and sweeps up the perpetrator, the victim and innocent bystanders in a vicious spiral of merciless destruction and impairment. There is little that is noble about violence. 'Each new morn', says Macduff of war in Shakespeare's Macbeth, 'New widows howl, new orphans cry, new sorrows Strike heaven in the face, that it resounds'.[1] And, yet, in democracies groups buffeted by all sorts of injustice opt for 'new sorrows' that strike heaven in the face.

In this chapter, I discuss precisely this problem: what the relationship between democracy and revolutionary violence is. In the second part of the chapter, I unpack different categories of violence and focus on state violence as well as revolutionary violence. The empirical referral for the discussion is revolutionary violence in Indian democracy.

Democracy and political violence: Unlikely companions

To many, the specific question whether in a democracy political violence as a form of politics that makes claims upon the body politic is justified might, of course, appear neither here nor there. Is not democracy, our interlocutors can indignantly ask, premised upon popular sovereignty? Is it not about free and fair elections, about accountability of representatives, about the consolidation of a solid political culture that permits debate and dissent and about institutions such as the judiciary that is bound to uphold the supremacy of constitutional rights? Why on earth should a group pick up arms and aim some very destructive weapons at agents of the state and members of society, when they have the right to articulate their politics through other means. Why should they transgress boundaries of what is politically permissible and legally sanctioned, and venture into dangerous territories, particularly when these transgressions are bound to create severe repercussions, and when they bode ill for the group in question?

To be fair, these hypothetical but irate responses to our question – why should we enquire whether political violence in a democracy is justified – are bang on track. In the field of logical reasoning, democracy and political violence are, or at least should be strangers to each other, ships that pass in the night with nary a nod to each other, the unknown and perhaps the unknowable. Democratic politics and violence, our interlocutors can insist inflexibly, simply do not inhabit the same conceptual and political universe.

They may be right. Democracy and violence can hardly be considered conceptual siblings, at least at first sight. The logic of each concept runs in different directions. Democracy enables citizens to come together across boundaries of class and ethnicity. The right to freedom of association, which is an essential precondition for the existence of a vibrant civil society brimming over with discussion, debate and contestation, is greatly conducive to the formation of dense networks of social associations. These associations may be philanthropic, or passionately concerned about the state of civil liberties in the country. Some may focus on the quality of national governance, and others might prefer to concentrate on local matters such as the dismal performance of neighbourhood schools. Some associations form fan clubs that lapse into delirium the moment superstars in films, or in soccer, or in cricket are mentioned, and others set up reading societies that solemnly and laboriously work out what a particular author or her work signifies. It matters little what specific objective associational life promotes, the simple pleasure of sociability, monitoring the state or keeping watch on uncivil groups in civil society. It is enough that an energetic civil society connects people who would have been otherwise locked into their own little worlds of isolation, sometimes permanently so.

Acts of violence, on the other hand, systematically and irrevocably separate, divide and segregate individuals and groups. These groups might have, till then, lived in some civility if not perfect harmony and neighbourliness. Violence positions them as combatants in a great divide. With a rapid flick of its long forked tongue, the serpent of violence poisons the environment, seeds an atmosphere of suspicion and terror, relentlessly casts a miasma of hate and doubt over communities and societies and destroys every hope that people sealed into circles of apprehension and fear may even consider initiating a conversation with others.

This is exactly what took place in Muzzafarnagar in India in early September 2013 when neighbour turned viciously on neighbour. 'They dismembered our people and raped our women' said Shoib, the inhabitant of a refugee camp for those who had managed to escape violence. Among the rioters were faces known to Shoib – faces of individuals whose family festivals he had routinely taken part in.[2] Similar stories of how people who had lived together as neighbours and co-workers for decades were transformed into vicious marauding mobs thirsting for their neighbour's blood have come to us from Bosnia, Kosovo, Sudan, from the struggle for the independence of Bangladesh and from the partition of India. The lesson is clear: there can be no truck and transaction let alone dialogue, between a group that is intent on, say, ethnic cleansing and the target group. The momentum of violence, that of sundering relationships, runs counter to that of democracy, which brings otherwise solitary people together in shared networks of associational life.

There are other deep differences between democracy and violence. Democracy enables people to route their aspirations, their demands and their expectations of the state through peaceful methods such as public gatherings, demonstrations, petitions, lobbying, campaigns, social networks, political movements, political theatrics and the media. Violence erupts outside these prescribed and institutionalized channels in public spaces, in cobbled streets, in forests and in inhospitable terrains. Democracy is guaranteed to secure the legitimacy of the state and of the holders of political power; political violence disputes the democratic credentials of the state. It also challenges the right of those who rule to, well, rule.

In short, violence negates, subverts and defies the fundamental presuppositions of democracy. And resting as it does on precepts of popular sovereignty and fundamental rights of citizens, freedom of debate and assembly and limited governments, democracy should logically rule out political violence. How can then democracy and violence live together in the same political or conceptual space, ever?

The coexistence of democracy and violent politics

Let us pause for a while at this point. Even though democracy and violence are antithetical concepts, they manage to coexist with each other in country after country. Can our committed democrats ignore this? Can they overlook the fact that violence has become a routine way of doing politics in countries like India? But that violence has become a routine way of doing politics in India is not the subject of great speculation. For example, there is a large body of literature on the successes of Indian democracy, and an equally large one on violence whether episodic or organized. Yet, studies, analysis, acclamation, condemnation and critical engagement with both concepts tend to wend their own literary, polemical, analytical, descriptive way with little prospect of intersection. It is almost as if it has been ordained that the twain shall not meet. Whether it has been ordained by the logic of democracy, or by the logic of violence, or both, is an open question.

Consider studies of democracy in India. Analysts and scholars celebrate, for undoubtedly very sound reasons, both the institutionalization of democracy in a highly unequal society and the dynamics that have been unleashed by this institutionalization. It is universally acknowledged that democracy has enabled the participation of groups that had been barred from the world of politics and political contestation among equals. The political agency of the so-called lower castes had been crippled by sometimes visible, sometimes invisible, but nevertheless highly effective systems of social prohibitions.

The codification of universal adult franchise as the linchpin of the Indian constitution has slackened these inhibiting social bonds. In the process, poor and predominantly poor, lower caste and rural voters have acquired political agency. They now exercise freedom of choice. In the sphere of electoral politics and in civil society, groups holding aloft their identity as members of this or that caste aggressively fight out issues of remedial justice. The fight for remedial justice forms part of a wider world of aspirations for equal status. The overturning of caste hierarchies in the electoral domain has marked a significant turning point in the way Indians think of themselves in relation to each other, and in relation to the state. In a society that has been for centuries deeply hierarchical, rigidly stratified and highly exclusionary, the institutionalization of the norm of universal adult franchise has proved nothing short of transformative.[3]

Despite the fact that India was at independence an unlikely candidate for democracy stamped as it was by poverty, illiteracy, irate caste and religious face offs and a deeply inegalitarian social order, the attraction of the *idea* of democracy (as distinct from the institutionalization of democracy) has proved durable. Over the years, we see the constitution of a body politic shaped by democratic imaginings and aspirations, and inspired by notions of equality. India, in short, has proved an exception to the rule that theorists of western democracy had up till now carved in stone, that is that democracy demands 'these' particular and not 'those' specific preconditions.

Unpacking political violence

India's record in maintaining democracy is undeniably impressive. At the same time, the biography of Indian democracy has been deeply scarred by violence. Apart from quotidian incidents of violence in the country such as road rage or domestic abuse, we can hardly put onto the back burner the spectre of major destruction that follows brutal and completely amoral terror attacks, crowds running amuck setting fire to public property, demonstrations that go painfully wrong and riots between caste and religious communities.

We can, of course, believe that murderous riots between religious and caste communities in India constitute exceptions to normal ways of being, and as disconnected occurrences, they signify periods of chaos and breakdowns. During riots, codes of civility, which otherwise earmark or at least should earmark practices of everyday life, are suspended, and norms and boundaries that govern social transactions are transgressed. We would have had very good reasons for our beliefs for some very insightful work in historical interpretation has told us that the riot constitutes departures from the norm.

Elias Cannetti focussing on destructive collective behaviour in his *Crowds and Power* suggests that such behaviour transgresses generally established and universally valid distances and boundaries, as well as destroys a hierarchy that is no longer recognized.[4] The implication seems to be that riots are little else than episodic and spasmodic events. But the breakdown of social codes is not permanent. These codes are put into abeyance for the time being and invariably restored when normalcy returns to the body politic. Riots have a short time span, and when the psychic high that is generated during the course of the riot is spent out, people return to ordinary ways of living with each other. Boundaries are restored to their rightful place. Yes, at one point of our history, we could have hoped that violent riots take place in a no-man's-land. In this space, neither the past nor the future is of the slightest consequence. Violence occurs in a time warp that mindlessly and meaninglessly constitutes a present: a present caught up in an admittedly vicious but nevertheless terminable spiral of violence. This is a reassuring thought; for then we could, with some ease, dismiss the riot as a contingent event marked by unreasonable crowd behaviour. In such situations, individual participants give into irrational impulses.

But, if we think of violence in this fashion, if we type this form of collective behaviour as an abnormality, we assume that the outbreak of violence has nothing to do with history, with social and political representations that profile communities and position them against each other, with competition in the economic and in the political marketplace or indeed, with the tensions which arise out of living together: tensions that permeate neighbourhoods and workplaces, rituals and public spaces. It is precisely here that we need to pause, reflect and wonder: does violence really signify isolated instances in human history abstracted both from the past and from the present?

We just have to dwell on the diverse and intricate ways in which violence is produced and reproduced in the body politic, to realize that violence, as a specific form of politics, is neither an aberration nor outside the provenance of democracy. Violence is not an unwelcome visitor, or an uninvited stranger who has strayed into our harmonious world, but whose prolonged stay can be brought to an end only if we, in a determined fashion, refuse to extend hospitality. On balance, we have to accept that violence is part of individual and collective lives. No matter how democratic a society may be, violence lurks on the sidelines, waiting for a cue to enter and wreck the carefully and painfully constructed democratic world where people see themselves as equal members of a political community.

In sum, the unhappy coexistence of democracy and violence cannot be wished away by neglecting either the context of violence that is democracy or ignoring the pervasiveness of violence in democracy. We can no longer see violence as an aberration, or see democracy as a gigantic fraud that is perpetuated upon political innocents. Most democracies are deeply flawed but they have nonetheless several achievements to their credit. Unless we wish to engage in the time-consuming and ultimately thankless task of constructing binary opposites: violent democracy versus democracy where violence is, but, an aberration, we have to look for a relationship from within democracy itself.

The prevalence of violence in democratic politics might well compel us acknowledge that democracy and violence inhabit the same political space. I am by no means arguing that democracy is embedded in violence. I suggest that we begin to think through the phenomenon of political violence and also reflect on how it relates to the fundamental presuppositions of democracy notably democratic justice. I explore this issue in Chapter 4, here let me merely suggest that the relationship cannot be one of exteriority; the links that bind democracy and violence have to be internal; they have to do with injustice. Nothing else explains the wide prevalence of violence in democratic life.

Violence is not a matter only for conflict theorists or for strategic and security studies; it is a matter for those who study and value democracy and justice. Something must have gone wrong, somewhere. We have to come to terms with the flaws in democracy, the lapses in democratic life and the imperfectability of democratic justice. We have to come to terms with violence within democracy.

Categories of violence

Violence seems to have become the defining feature of Indian society as in other countries. Headlines of morning newspapers regularly disburse news about the latest incident, of often incredible brutality, etched onto the bodies of women, of children, of the so-called lower castes and minority groups and of others with deadly knife slashes. At any given day and time, everyday violence ranges from child abuse, to female foeticide, gang rapes, acid attacks on women, road rage, criminal acts for personal benefits, to the sort of violence that vulnerable sections of society, such as domestic and bonded labour, are subjected to. Though all categories of violence are political because violence is an act of power, assertion of domination and the extraction of subordination, let us talk about specifically political violence.

In a preliminary way, let us note the main characteristics of political violence. First, the concept of political violence enables us to distinguish organized forms of violence from sporadic and uncoordinated protests, and other manifestations of public anger that lead to arson, destruction of property and loss of lives. Second, political violence is unleashed in the public domain. Third, the agents of political violence are ideologically charged groups. Individuals commit acts of violence, for example suicide bombers. However, these individuals, either implicitly or explicitly, are bearers of an ideology. Andres Behring Breivik shot seventy-seven people on the island of Utoeya as an act of protest against the Norwegian government's immigration policy. The violence was individually executed, notably however, the perpetrator was embedded in an ideology of race discrimination.

In India, similar ideologies of exclusion and discrimination have motivated groups to inflict savage violence on the heads of minority or vulnerable ethnic groups. Ahmedabad (1969), Belchi (1978), anti-Sikh riots in Delhi (1984), Bombay riots (1993), Bathan Tola (1996), Laxman Bathe (1997), Gujarat (2002), Kherlainji (2006), Dharmapuri

(2012) and Muzzafarnagar (2013). These are not only names given to places on the map of India. They signify milestones in the sordid biography of communal and caste, or simply ethnic violence in India. History will tell a blood-soaked story of shameful incidents in the country, of inhuman acts performed by one human being on another for reasons outside the latter's control-birth into a particular ethnic community.

Of course, other ignoble motives underpin ethnic riots, such as attempts to grab remunerative land or the settling of personal scores. Running like a strong skein through these incidents is another story: that of struggle for power. These incidents of violence are not random or abstracted from deeper struggles over power in society. They are, indeed, signifiers of these struggles. For ethnic violence throws onto the political horizon the one question that is crucial to democracy – the relative standing of persons in society. The aim of ethnic riots is to redraw the normative map drafted by democracies and constitutions: that of equality of political status irrespective of religion, caste, ethnicity, gender and class. It appears that those who wield violent weapons are in the business of warning others, those others who would dare to subvert social hierarchies that in some societies are considered ordained by the law of nature. Ethnic violence seeks to restore an older social order based on hierarchy and exclusion, domination and subordination, and dispense with the new democratic order that upholds as an organizing principle of the political community the principles of non-discrimination and equality.

The institutionalization of political equality in countries of the global south, vide social movements and constitutions, has actually succeeded in a strange way. It has bred uncertainty and fear among social groups who believe that they and they alone have the right to dominate others by reasons of birth into a particular religion, class, caste or for that matter gender. Struggles in the arena of ethnic, class and gender politics are struggles over which group occupies what status in society. Equality of status is a relational concept; therefore, dominant elites contest hotly ideas that other ethnic groups are as equal as they are. Violence in this case erupts over claims to universal rights of equality, freedom and justice. Ethnic violence inscribes in fine and painful detail the way groups resist the institutionalization of a new and equitable political order, and the way the targeted groups fight for this order. For this reason, this avatar of inter-group violence falls within the category of political violence.

A second category of political violence is employed to make demands upon the state and force changes in policy. Some groups use violence strategically in order to wrest collective benefits from the state ranging from, say, the extension of affirmative action policies to 'this' or 'that' group, to the demand for a separate state within the federal system. Collective benefits are wrested from the state through the use of violence.

Third, a group might resort to violence because it wants to simply opt out and establish a state of its own. This sort of political violence falls into a distinct category. Groups that want benefits from the state neither challenge state legitimacy nor renounce political obligation. They can hardly do that because they expect the state to provide the goods on demand. They do not renege on political obligation. Notably, they renege on moral obligation to their fellow citizens, because violence is used to prise open the economic and the political coffers of the state for the benefit of one section of citizens alone.

Secessionists, on the other hand, renege on both political and moral obligation. They renounce the sovereignty of the state and wish to establish a new one forged out of the territory and the people of the existing state. They also renege on moral obligation to the citizens of the state they wish to secede from in so far as they make it quite clear that they do not owe anything to them. Keep your society unequal, corrupt, exploitative and rotten, they seem to say, just give us a state of our own. Secession raises a profound dilemma for most of us. Is it politically prudent to support a leadership that skilfully deploys violence to acquire advantages for only the members of its own constituency, a constituency that has been forged through deliberate political fashioning and one that is based on notions of who belongs and who does not belong. On balance, these notions are grounded in ethnic affiliations. It follows that people who have not been born into that particular community are excluded by definitional fiat. It is precisely the abdication of moral obligation to people who do not belong to the right, ethnic group even if they are in want; that makes it difficult to unconditionally defend the use of secessionist violence.[5]

The complexities of revolutionary violence

The issue is much more complex in the fourth case: revolutionary violence, which forms the subject matter for this work. Revolutionaries seek to transform the institutional context in which people live out their lives and make it less unequal and more just, through armed struggle which has as its long-term objective the takeover of the state. This avatar of violence can be distinguished from other forms in distinctive ways. It does not seek to wrest collective benefits from the state. That is, the proponents of this form of politics do not see violence as a way of making demands upon the state. This course of action implies that the state is legitimate, and that it can deliver benefits to citizens if pushed hard enough.

The proponents of revolutionary violence believe, on the other hand, that the state is not only unwilling, but incapable of institutionalizing the basic preconditions of justice for the most vulnerable: through, say, redistribution of resources, guarantees of a life of dignity and assurances that the political voice of people who are trapped in the clutches of injustices will be heard. The chains that tie different forms of injustice are durable and inflexible. Injustice carries no expiry date. The tangle of injustice can be untangled only through violence, and ultimately the replacement of the state by one that belongs to the people.

Unlike secessionist politics, revolutionary violence does not seek to break away a piece of a territory of the existing state and establish a new state in the name of a particular ethnic or religious group. The group wielding revolutionary violence reneges on political obligation to the state, but not on moral obligation to fellow citizens, particularly the most deprived, the most discriminated against, the most oppressed, and the most exploited and in general those who are victims of a history not of their making.

Revolutionary groups do not say 'keep your state and society, rotten, corrupt, unequal, exploitative and unjust as it is' all we want is a state of our own. They seek to replace a state that has displayed remarkable and a somewhat stunning incapacity and unwillingness to provide justice to its citizens with a state that will be responsive to precisely those people that have been consigned to the footpaths and the ditches of the road during the long march of history. This is the objective of violence in the revolutionary mode.

More importantly, revolutionary violence is based less upon the use of instruments of force and destruction and more on political mobilization of the group of peasants on whose behalf the guerrillas have picked up arms, and in influencing public opinion. The war against recalcitrant elites is political rather than military in so far as the objective is to build up a political movement that recognizes that society is embedded in injustice, that the state is the codified power of the social formation and that all manifestations of injustice have to be battled, transformed and made receptive to the voice of those people who have been banished to the fringes. The task is not easy given the intractability and inflexibility of power relations. If political strategies short of violence have not succeeded in unshackling the lives of people from necessity, violence has to be used to break these bonds. Violence, as the time honoured adage holds, has to be the midwife of history. There is no other option in revolutionary politics.

Revolutionary politics in a different vein

Of course, revolutions have not always been made by or even on behalf of poor peasants. Barrington Moore in his classic work on the social origins of dictatorship and democracy explored the varied political roles played by landed upper classes and the peasantry in the transformation from agrarian societies to modern industrial ones.[6] Different societies, he suggested, took different routes towards the making of a modern industrial society, and discrete complexes of historical factors enabled specific classes to play a significant role in the transition. The complex of these factors produced different outcomes. For instance, the Puritan revolution in England, the French Revolution and the American Civil War created the political context for bourgeois revolutions. These revolutions gave political expression to deep-rooted economic changes that had already taken place, such as the rise of the bourgeois class, decline of the power of the landlords and the seminal shift in the social basis of the state. Bourgeois revolutions heralded not only a new economic dispensation, but also a new political order marked by constitutionalism, limited government and the grant of basic fundamental rights to citizens. The outcome institutionalized both capitalism and parliamentary democracy.

In Germany and Japan in the late nineteenth century, modernizing revolutions were crafted by a landlord class, more than conscious of the need for transforming the economy into a modern industrial one. The role of this class was central to 'revolutions from above', simply because the bourgeois impulse was weak, and the peasantry was equally weak. Though the revolutionary path to a modern society also led to capitalism, given the absence of a strong revolutionary surge, it passed through reactionary political forms and culminated in fascism. That is, though 'revolutions from above' transformed the economics of these two countries, economic modernization did not lead to a liberal democratic political order of the kind witnessed in countries that had undergone bourgeois revolutions.

Moore contrasted 'revolutions from above' with what he called 'revolutions from below' that took place in China and in Russia. In both countries, the bourgeois impulse was weak. However, agrarian class relations were marked by conflict, and this factor enabled the politicization of the peasantry. Semi-imperialism had greatly weakened the state in China and made it dependent on the landlord class, both to maintain control over the peasantry and to ensure production. The intensification of repression on the peasantry deepened political consciousness among the class. Political mobilization by the Chinese Communist Party, which tapped memories of large-scale peasant rebellions, radicalized an already politically aware peasantry and forged a revolutionary moment. The revolution targeted both imperialism and feudalism. In Russia and in China, revolutions had their exclusive origins in the peasantry, and this factor alone made communism possible.[7]

The one country, which Moore thought should have had a revolution, but which failed on this front, is India. Despite wide-scale poverty and misery, India had not experienced a bourgeois revolution. Nor had it experienced a conservative revolution from above, or indeed a communist one. The impact of colonialism on the country had resulted in a weak bourgeois impulse and a large but conservative peasantry. Both these factors contributed to a non-revolutionary situation.

Moore published his magisterial work in 1966, and barely a year later, the Naxal revolution broke out in West Bengal. The revolutionary movement persists till today, in some form or the other, fragmented at one time, and united in another, as we shall see in Chapter 3. Moore was correct in one respect though. The revolutionary *movement* continues to throw light on the infirmities of Indian democracy, on inequality and on poverty, but the time for a revolutionary *moment* has still not come around. The reasons for this lag between a revolutionary *movement* and a revolutionary *moment* are discussed in Chapter 5. Perhaps the lag has to do with the political context of revolutionary violence – democracy howsoever imperfectly institutionalized democratic justice maybe. The paradox is that revolutionary violence has flared up in imperfectly just democracies like India, but the democratic context inhibits the realization of the objectives of this brand of politics, but more on this anon. Let me now thread the argument above and try to arrive at a comprehensive definition of political violence.

The two faces of violence

Political violence is practised by organized and ideologically charged groups that seek to impact the political order in some way, to stake a claim on the political order, to change it or indeed to defend it. The last part of the definition enables us to conceive of states and/or vigilante groups that act on behalf of the state as agents of political violence. Non-state groups use political violence to make demands on the body politic. The state is also guilty of using political violence to resist these demands, and of hammering the polity and society in a particular shape and form through law and the use of coercion. Let me illustrate this with reference to an incident in India's recent history.

On 26 May 2013, India's revolutionary guerrillas, the Maoists, ambushed a string of cars ferrying leaders of the Congress party in the Bastar forests of Chattisgarh and attacked passengers. Twenty-eight persons were killed. The Indian security establishment promptly went off into paroxysms of acute hysteria. So did self-appointed spokespersons of 'Indian' public opinion. Strident demands to exterminate 'terrorists' and 'terrorism' assaulted our collective eardrums once again. On a less hysterical note, a number of security experts reiterated that the latest Maoist attempt on the life of political figures was deplorable, and that it was time the Indian state did something about this most serious threat to the security of the country. It should use all the means of destruction at its command to exterminate the Maoists.

Public indignation mounted at reports of how the Maoists sprayed bullets on the occupants of cars, how they targeted Mahendra Karma popularly known as the Bastar tiger and how they subjected him to unspeakable acts of violence. Eyewitnesses told the media that Karma's hands were tied behind his back, that he was taken into a thicket and that a female cadre of the Maoists shot him at close range. Other women cadres stabbed him seventy-eight times with their bayonets. Reportedly, they executed a macabre dance of death on his body, kicked it around like a beach ball and abandoned it.

Senseless acts of violence performed on a dead man by cadres of a political formation, even one that declares itself wedded to violence as creed and as political strategy, repelled and repelled thoroughly. The widespread and insistent demand that the Maoists should be simply wiped out appears warranted, indeed the paramount need of the hour.

Let us, however, tarry for a moment and glance briefly at the context in which these senseless and brutal killings had occurred. The way Mahendra Karma was tortured and killed, and his body desecrated, gives us enough reason to erupt in vociferous indignation. At the same time, one could not help but remember that this man, who represented Bastar in the popular house of the Indian Parliament, and Dantewada in the state assembly, was responsible for the founding of two rabidly anti-Maoist forces in the state of Chattisgarh: Jan Jagran Abhiyan in the 1990s and the infamous Salwa Judum in 2005.

Salwa Judum, a notorious vigilante group supported by the state government and funded by the central government, forcibly moved thousands of tribals from their homes and relocated them in camps, ostensibly for the purposes of protecting them against the Maoists. This was borne out by the 2009 Report of Sub-Group IV of the central government appointed 'Committee on State Agrarian Relations and Unfinished Task of Land Reform'. The report confirmed that the vigilante group was created and encouraged by the state government, was supported by the armouries of the central government and was trained in organisational skills by the security forces of the state.

This state-funded privately armed group, writes Jason Miklian, represented itself as a popular movement against Maoism. A deeper and ignoble conspiracy was, however, afoot. The leaders of Salwa Judum, or rather war-lords, proceeded to divide the territory and the forest resources of Dantewada amongst themselves. They controlled camps sheltering displaced persons, displaced in the first instance by these very leaders. In exchange for protection services, they received funding, food and arms from the Chattisgarh state. Convoys of trucks carried war lords, who were protected by automatic weapon-wielding plainclothes and security personnel, across the length and breadth of the region of Dantewada. The idea was to recruit young men as special police officers or supplementary forces. These war lords unleashed a reign of terror on the region in order to accomplish their aims.[8]

In addition to garnering profits for its members, the organization had been contracted by corporates intent on appropriating mineral-rich land, in order to provide protection and ground-clearing services for excavation and mining.[9] Not surprisingly, these activities bore a bitter harvest. Villagers were displaced, villages were stripped bare, vast stretches of cultivable land lay fallow, collection of forest produce was disrupted, people had no access to weekly markets, schools were turned into police camps and basic rights were trampled upon.[10] Not surprisingly, the criminal acts of the S.J. drove many a young tribal into the arms of the Maoists.

A petition was filed in the Supreme Court by scholars and activists requesting that the court ensures that the state government discontinue its support of the vigilante group consisting of more than 5,000 tribal youths. On 5 July 2011, the Supreme Court ordered that both the Chattisgarh government and the central government should desist from arming callow youth, and allotting to them the status of Special Police Officers expected to perform police functions. Raw recruits had neither been given basic training in the use of arms, nor rudimentary knowledge of human rights law. And, these hurriedly conscripted young men had been let loose on villagers in the name of fighting Maoism by any means possible.[11]

We might also do well to remember that in the months preceding the attack on the convoy of Congress leaders, the state government had majorly hyped up military operations against the Maoists. The paramilitary organization of the government, the Central Reserve Police Force, set up bases in areas of Bastar considered to be Maoist strongholds and took over health centres and schools. From here the force not only launched sorties to flush out Maoists from the forests, but also terrorized local populations.

It is possible to recount story after story of the competitive violence unleashed by the government, the Maoists and vigilante groups on the inhabitants in the region named the 'Red Corridor' in central and eastern India. We can tell another story of how both perpetrators and victims have been scooped up in the maelstrom of violence to such an extent that their identities have fused. The victim has become the perpetrator, and those who inflict violence have been reduced to objects of target practice. But that is another story.

This story is about the acute political dilemma that confronts those who try to think beyond the obvious and the banal. The Maoists have let loose a fury of violence on innocent citizens who travel in trains that blow up, who inadvertently walk or drive over landmines placed by guerrilla bands of the party, and are thereby consigned to oblivion, who are caught fatally in the crossfire between the armed guerrillas and the security forces of the state, and who inhabiting the region the Maoists have made their base, live in constant fear that they will be targeted as informers or police agents, and executed by kangaroo courts. Coercion, intimidation and strong-arm tactics are outrageous and condemnable. These acts violate our basic moral sensibilities and violate deeply held convictions that the least that is due to human beings is respect for the right to life, howsoever stark that life may be.

Do we find the overreach of state violence, and state sponsored violence, quite so outrageous and condemnable? On the 26 of January every year, India celebrates the anniversary of that momentous day in 1950 when the country was constituted politically as a Republic. The Indian state showcases the country's plural and diverse culture through dance, music and visual representations. Exotically designed floats representing the traditions and history of regions are, undeniably, the high point of the Republic Day parade. Also trotted out with some conceit is the country's formidable arsenal of violence, garnished in the colours of the great Indian Republic that has promised to its people justice, social, economic and political, in the preamble of the constitution.

How many of us wonder whether some of these weapons are fated to be turned on our own people: dissenters in the valley of Kashmir, insurgents in substantial parts of the North-East and people living in regions considered Maoist strongholds? India is considered the world's largest democracy, and this is certainly a matter for gratification. But for some decades now, we have seen with regret the increasing and arbitrary use of force against citizens in the form of encounter deaths, police torture, firing on peaceful demonstrations, charges and the ferocious use of water cannons against young people who dare to protest against sexual violence unleashed on women in the streets of Delhi, unwarranted arrests and detention and suspension of basic civil liberties in major parts of the country.

State violence

In the Kashmir Valley, and in parts of the North East, the Indian state has come to be known as the harbinger of death and destruction. Firing on peaceful protests, killing of suspects, rapes and torture have become the hallmark of the power that security forces command, even as they occupy the valley. The ruthlessness with which inhabitants of regions typed the Maoist 'Red Corridor' are treated is scandalous and shameful. And the democratic state makes absolutely no attempt to remedy its own record as a violator of basic human rights. The number of stories that compose the long and sordid narrative of state violence in India is beyond belief.

Despite a plethora of human rights legislation, India has one of the worst records in human rights. According to the 'Status Report 2012-Human Rights in India' released by the Working Group on Human Rights (convenor Miloon Kothari) of the United Nations Human Rights Commission, the Government of India has rejected the recommendation that it should ratify the Convention Against Torture. The GOI also rejected the recommendation that draconian laws like the Armed Forces Special Powers Act that provides immunity to the army in cases of human rights violations should be reviewed and repealed, so that it is aligned with the obligations of the government under the International Covenant on Civil Rights.

Despite claims that the Indian government ritually trots out that it faces neither international nor non-state conflict in what is called insurgent zones, security forces have been held responsible by civil rights organizations, by independent tribunals and by the Supreme Court, for disappearances, arbitrary arrests, torture, extra-judicial killings, sexual violence and use of lethal force to disperse crowds agitating against state-sponsored violence. India still has to accept the recommendation of the UNHRC that capital punishment should be outlawed. Human rights are persistently violated by the state, concluded the report. The number of Indian citizens killed in the name of national security, territorial integrity, the war against terror and other acts construed as national crimes is beyond calculation. We do not even know the extent of harm committed in the name of some or the other unspecified national interest.

Extra-judicial killings of people whose guilt has yet to be established in a court of law, and whose complicity in some or the other crime is highly debatable, are accepted by citizens, by the media and by representatives with a degree of unthinking ease. Policemen popularly known as 'encounter specialists' are celebrated, rewarded and immortalized by the Bombay film industry. Take the case of Dayanand Nayak, a police sub-inspector of the Bombay police, who reportedly killed more than fifty gangsters during his career. The 'fame' that he had carved out for himself through extra-judicial killings was chronicled and acclaimed in the 2004 movie 'Ab Tak Chappan' produced by Ram Gopal Varma and directed by Shimit Amin. Increasingly, movies have begun to commemorate vigilantes who kill in the name of national security, an interesting departure from the one-man army of Amitabh Bachan intent on extracting revenge from some individual that had wronged him and his family in the past. Vigilantes do not only kill to sort out personal traumas, but they kill to rid the country of, as the gifted actor Naseeruddin

Shah put it in the Neeraj Pandey 2008 directed thriller *A Wednesday*, 'cockroaches' who infiltrate society bringing with them disease and pestilence.

India is not alone in accepting state violence as a given. Few eyebrows are raised at the indiscriminate and lawless excesses committed by the police, paramilitary forces, the army and by vigilante groups the world over. Ideologies of security, territorial integrity and the war against terror have bludgeoned societies into complacency and acceptance of state violence. Humankind has become insensitive to violence and to the harm that attends politics in this mode. If in a democracy people are arbitrarily imprisoned, tortured and killed, this should be a matter of public outrage, of concern and of demands for the resignation of the government that has violated the fundamental maxim of a constitutional contract between the state and the political public. The political tragedy is that state violence, for the most part, goes unremarked. All this, and nary an explanation, or any sort of justification for the indiscriminate violence that citizens are subjected to, except in the tired and overused language of state security.

That democratic states unleash realms of violence on their own citizens is indisputably condemnable. But I do not elaborate more on this phenomenon. I take it as a given that even democratic states are condensates of power, that these states do not hesitate from inflicting harm on their own citizens and that they have the resources to garner support among the political public for such actions. More interesting are questions of how people speak back to the state, more interesting is the issue of agency and more interesting is the issue of why revolutionary politics cannot promote agency.

Shall we speak of violence?

Given the widespread resort to violence as a form of political claim-making and political rejection, there is some need to speak of political violence, to open up the phenomenon to scrutiny, to distinguish between various forms of political violence and to approach everyday vocabularies and newspaper headlines with the proverbial pinch of salt.

Who would not accept that a world without violence is infinitely preferable to a world of violence? But we inhabit imperfect and flawed societies. The promises of democracy remain unrealized. And the norms of justice are destined to be unfulfilled. We do not have to be votaries of violence to comprehend why people who suffer from historical injustices such as extreme economic deprivation, social stigma that refuses erasure, state-sponsored coercion and lack of voice in the public domain of civil society resort to violence. In such contexts, violence can conceivably become its own justification, sometimes, somewhat, perhaps a weapon of the last resort, but also indispensable in situations of extreme disadvantage.

No less a person than Gandhi, the paramount apostle of non-violence, accepted that violence in certain conditions is unavoidable. Violence, he once remarked at a public meeting, was certainly preferable to cowardice. 'I would rather have India resort to arms in order to defend her honour than that she should in a cowardly manner become or remain a helpless witness to her own dishonour.'[12] For Gandhi not only is violence preferable compared to lesser or inferior sentiments such as cowardice, it can be defended if it prevents greater harm. In some circumstances, 'taking life may be a duty... We do destroy as much life as we think necessary for sustaining the body... Even manslaughter may be necessary in certain cases. Suppose a man runs amuck and goes furiously sword in hand, killing anyone that comes in his way, and no one dares to capture him alive. Anyone who despatches this lunatic will earn the gratitude of the community and be regarded as a benevolent man'.[13] Finally, Gandhi suggested that it is violence to cause suffering to others out of our selfishness, or just for the sake of doing so. But if it is necessary to cause suffering to make someone happy, dispassionately and unselfishly, this is non-violence. There is a distinction between the act of injuring a thief to save oneself and injuries produced by a doctor to bring relief.[14]

Gandhi's endorsement of violence is conditional and contextual; that is the context and/or intent justifies or does not justify the use of violence. In a similar fashion, let us, at least, begin to ask the following question. When groups neither hope nor expect justice for harm done, is violence by non-state actors prima facie justified? Dare we harbour the thought that non-state actors are, on the face of it, justified in using violence because they have reached the nadir of desperation, or because violence for them represents the ultimate and perhaps the final act of protest, or because violence enables to recover political agency that the state and dominant classes have sought to obliterate or because violence is the midwife to a new society?

Can we move beyond hegemonic beliefs and speculate who these people are. What are the personal biographies of people who are fated to be massacred by the security forces of the state or blown up in landmine explosions detonated by Maoists? Equally, why did some groups pick up the nearest weapon and aim it against the state and minions? Did they lose hope and trust in India's democracy completely, or did they never have cause to hope and to trust in the first place? Do we, who occupy privileged places in society, ever wonder what it is like to be relentlessly hunted down, tortured and killed? Can we empathize with the fact that the hunted will at some point of time turn on the hunter in order to reverse the order of domination? This can happen even in democracy, because we have found that justice does not always follow the route of democracy. On the contrary, democracy provides us with the space to struggle for the realization of justice. Some of these struggles have to use violence in order to do so.

Therefore, let us begin to think about the issue of violence in public life contextually. Little attention has been paid to these questions because the very idea that non-state actors, in certain and specified circumstances, are entitled to use violence is ruled out by definitional fiat. Political discourses whether of the state or of civil society tend to dismiss armed struggle against injustice as terrorism or as a law and order problem. In the process, we often take the side of coercive states.

Conclusion

All this makes the task of exploring various dimensions of revolutionary violence daunting. Nevertheless, we have to take it on because increasingly groups in India and other countries tend to see violence as a form of doing politics. We need to sort out different forms of violence and see which is worthy of a limited and provisional defence, and which is not. Before taking on this task of sorting out the untidiness of political violence, the concept of violence, which has arguably been overextended by a number of different authors and experts, needs to be clarified, somewhat. Though we are fairly certain that we recognize violence when we see or experience it, it is undoubtedly one of the most knotty of concepts that political theorists have to deal with. It is to this discussion that I turn.

The Many Shades of Violence

Introduction

Of what is it that we speak when we speak of 'violence'? The term possesses a great deal of rhetorical value, commands immediate attention and evokes strong reactions ranging from reluctant fascination, to shock, to revulsion and to disapproval. In the lexicon of the English language, the status of violence as an impact-word is, perhaps, unrivalled. Maybe that is why violence comes so readily onto our lips and trips so easily from our tongue. We tend to readily reach for the word/term 'violence' and disregard the fact that other words, which might capture and conceptualize a state of affairs clearly and more precisely, are also readily available. Think of moments when we began to describe an incident to a friend, for example, that Ram subjected his spouse Rati to a string of choice epithets. It is more than likely that we will use the term 'violent' instead of abusive when we stick a descriptive label onto Ram's speech.

Words, of course, are tricky things and we can never be sure/certain/confident/ assured that we have used the right word to express/convey what we wanted to say. An interesting exchange between Alice and Humpty Dumpty in *Through the Looking Glass* might illustrate what I am trying to say. 'I don't know what you mean by "glory"?' said Alice to Humpty Dumpty. The latter smiled contemptuously, 'of course you don't – till I tell you. I meant there's a nice knock-down argument for you!' 'But "glory" doesn't mean "a nice down argument"', Alice objected. 'When I use a word', Humpty Dumpty said scornfully, 'it means just what I choose it to mean – neither more nor less'. 'The question is', said Alice, 'whether you can make words mean so many different things'. 'The question is', said Humpty Dumpty, 'which is to be master-that's all'.

Lewis Carroll, mathematician and logician, excelled in the subtle art of satire and word play. Coded in this exchange between Alice and Humpty Dumpty, which appears a piece of delightful literary nonsense at first sight, is a message. The search for unequivocal meaning, Carroll seems to tell us, is doomed. Speakers intend that their words should mean more or less what they want them to mean. And readers or listeners interpret these words/sentences/paragraphs through their own prism of understanding. Within a given range, the term 'violence' can be infused with any one of the several meanings the author/ speaker wishes to attribute to the term, ranging from intimidation, abuse, brutality, force, coercion, to harassment.

But we dwell too much on this point, and for this particular argument the point is relatively minor. The extensive and often unnecessary use of violence in everyday speech is hardly a matter of immense significance. In the hands of a skilled speaker, inclined towards extravagant propositions and fulsome overstatements, the substitution of violence for other words can be used tellingly and to dramatic effect. Violence is after all a high-impact word. There is absolutely nothing wrong here. We seldom choose the words we use with care and after considerable deliberation. That would prove fatal for whatever spontaneity or conversational skills we possess. Instinctively, though, we seem to know which word sounds better, or more effective, in a sequence of words we call a sentence.

When, however, the *concept* of violence becomes a stand-in for other concepts, which are infinitely more suitable simply because they illumine both the issue at hand and the implications that follow with greater clarity, it is time to wonder what this substitution does to conceptual understanding. It is a sad reflection on the present state of political science, wrote the great philosopher Hannah Arendt (1906–1975), that our terminological language does not distinguish between key terms such as power, strength, force, authority and violence, all of which refer to distinct, different phenomena and would hardly exist unless they did. To use them as synonyms, she suggested, indicates not only certain deafness to linguistic meaning, it has also resulted in blindness with respect to the realities they correspond to.

Her essay on violence published in 1969 bore the stamp of the times, the cold war, the nuclear arms race, American intervention in Vietnam and above all campus and worker revolts in Europe and the United States. The late 1960s and the early 1970s witnessed substantial outpourings of philosophical literature as political philosophers rushed to think through what violence means, and what it stands for. And this was the urgent need of the day, for large numbers of students, activists and workers inspired by the Maoist dictum that power flows out of the barrel of a gun had revolted against the system and opted for violence.

In this context, Arendt set out to distinguish power from violence. Power, she argued, exerts a moral force. For this very reason violence cannot generate power. To make precisely this point, she warned against the practice of using violence either as a catch-all term or as a synonym for other more apt concepts. We cannot reduce, she argued, public affairs to dominion.[1]

From a related vantage point, let me add to the critique of the indiscriminate use of the concept of violence, a concept that is explanatory, descriptive, normative, or all three. How does the substitution of violence for other terms help us comprehend the specific ways in which people are harmed? How does this switch help us to grasp the implications of specific forms of injustice? This work tries to negotiate these questions as part of a political project, of advancing the cause of justice. Simply put, in order to press for remedial justice, we have to be sure of what sort of injustice has been inflicted upon groups of people.

One objective of the argument in the second part of this chapter is to try to distinguish violence from other sorts of injustices. But before that we have to grapple with the many shades of violence, simply in order to establish the meaning attributed to violence in this essay. Since one of the tasks of a political theorist is to strive towards conceptual clarity, I explore some influential understandings and interpretations of violence and proceed to define what is meant by violence.

Overloading violence

We must know what we speak of when we speak of violence, simply because the concept has become a hot favourite of a number of influential theorists, particularly those belonging to the left. In the process, it has been subjected to some degree of over-extension. It has simply imploded. We no longer seem to know what the difference between torture in the police stations of Delhi and little babies dying of malnutrition in remote areas of India is.

Take the concept of structural violence, which has taken on a new lease of life after the intellectual labours of Giorgio Agamben and Slavoj Žižek. The anthropologist Akhil Gupta in a fascinating work on the arbitrariness and the randomness, with which the lower bureaucracy treats groups targeted by poverty eradication programmes, argues that structural violence is responsible for the paradox of Indian politics. The paradox is that huge numbers of Indians remain mired in poverty despite a plethora of anti-poverty programmes. Gupta makes the usual nod to Agamben but chooses to rely heavily on the Norwegian sociologist Johann Galtung's articulation of the concept.

In 1969, amidst a profusion of writings on violence, the concept of structural violence had been popularized by Johann Galtung. Galtung was interested in violence because he was interested in peace. Basically, he expanded the concept of violence to include injustice. A society in which no one physically harms another human is peaceful, but only in a negative sense. Positive peace can be obtained when structural violence, embedded in unjust social and political institutions and practices, is banished. Structural violence is not direct, nor can it be attributed to identifiable individuals, but the net impact of this genre of violence is the same as that of visible and targeted acts. Structural violence impedes the somatic and mental realisations of human beings.[2] Direct violence causes harm. Injustice also causes harm. The similarity in outcomes puts both violence and injustice into the same category of structural violence.

Galtung seems to suggest that nothing less than the realisation of justice secures peace. The identification of two different sorts of objectives, howsoever desirable they may be, is, however, a little puzzling. We can easily subscribe to the proposition that justice can be realized only when that society is (relatively) peaceful, or that peace is a necessary precondition of justice, not its synonym. Scholars have identified other problems with Galtung's theory of structural violence,[3] but here let us turn to Akhil Gupta and see how he conceptualizes structural violence.[4] Gupta is concerned with invisible forms of violence in India, such as poverty that leads to the death of millions of the poor, especially women, girls, lower-caste people and indigenous people. Poverty is crippling because it prevents people from doing what they should be doing or what they want to do. It can, therefore, be seen as a case of structural violence. The unarticulated analogy is with physical violence. P by injuring Q prevents the latter from performing actions that make her life worthwhile. But, poverty prevents people from actualizing their capacities. Gupta's notion of structural violence goes much beyond physical injury; it includes exclusions from entitlements such as food and water, and also the exclusion of certain groups from particular forms of recognition such as citizenship rights, equal rights before the law, right to education and representation.

Faithful to Galtung, Gupta argues structural violence that produces victims and triggers suffering cannot be attributed to a particular agent. It represents in Gupta's memorable words a 'crime without a criminal'. But even though the identity of the criminal cannot be latched onto with precision, generally speaking, everyone who benefits from the system is complicit in the perpetration of structural violence on those who do not benefit. Expectedly, the doers of violence in India include not only the elites, but also the fast-growing middle class, whose increasing number and great consumer power are celebrated by an aggressive 'global capitalism'.[5] Certain classes of people have a stake in perpetuating a social order in which extreme suffering is not only tolerated but also taken as normal. Evidently, there is no collective wish to change the status quo. Clearly, all those who are poor are victims, and all those who are not poor are purveyors of violence.

The proposition is bound to take lovers of detective fiction aback. A murder most foul has been committed, but there is no murderer whose identity the author of the novel will unfold only in the last pages of the detective story. Surely in cases of murder, or even serious physical injury, there must be an agent of violence, and there must be some sort of force that voluntarily or involuntarily involves coercion. How on earth did these victims come to harm? Gupta tells us that in order to answer this question we have to commit regicide.

That is we should unpack the state, decompose it into the myriads of constituents that comprise the institution and detect thereby the production of a culture of indifference. This culture is manifested through slippages, casualness and randomness with which targets of anti-poverty programmes are viewed. Bureaucratic casualness and arbitrariness guarantee not only that people live in dire want, but also that some sections of needy people win, and others, who are equally needy, lose out. Gupta's anthropology of the fragments of the Indian state explores the modalities of violence-corruption, modes of writing and governmentality. This is undeniably the strong point of the book. From the perspective of political theory, the focus on structural violence is also one of its possible weaknesses.

Maximal notions of violence

Consider the currently fashionable concept of structural violence, at once both theatrical and imprecise. As an expansive notion of violence, it can mean anything, from the production of violence by social orders to the production of social orders by violence. Violence does not have a beginning, a mid-point or an end. It is part of institutions, practices and culture, embedded in the very woodwork that frames the life of the social collective. Certainly, the ascription of violence to the intricate and confusing pirouettes of capitalism produces an argument that is both appealing and persuasive. Why should we only see police brutality as an instance of violence that is attended by great harm, but not see artificially created food shortages that cripple little children, or damage expectant and lactating mothers, as violence? All too often cases of direct and transparent violence get precedence in news reports, and malnutrition is seen as the product of a malfunctioning system. Admittedly, the imaginary produced by the concept of structural violence is deeply persuasive. It has convinced many a friend on the left that capitalism and violence are conjoined at the hip, Siamese twins no less.

Yet doubts remain, simply because the expansion of a concept beyond recognizable boundaries can also loosen it out to an alarming degree. Nuclear war that kills millions and irremediably scars generations to come represents a straightforward case of violence. This is clear. Do great divergences in income also represent a case of structural violence, or do they properly belong to another category, say inequality and injustice? I will come back to this later in this section of the argument, here let us explore some of the other weaknesses of what, otherwise is a powerful, even a seductive political argument.

First, is nothing going on in society outside the frame of violence? Second, are these theorists using violence descriptively or conceptually? Third, do structures predetermine action or do we impact structures by our actions? Indisputably, structures inhibit individual actions, for example patriarchy seriously hampers the capacity of women to live lives the way they want to. On the other hand, the institution of patriarchy has been impacted by the rise of the feminist movement, and by the way the movement has shaped the political consciousness of women and some men. Structures constrain but they also enable.

These are interesting questions and worth exploring, but it seems to me that the problem with theories of structural violence lies elsewhere. The concept simply does not distinguish between intentional violence and violence as the unintended outcome of a host of other factors. But there may be, and often is, a qualitative distinction between the two. Consider the case of a government that has taken on the responsibility of providing reasonably priced food to poor citizens. But food just does not reach this segment of the population. Failure to ensure that people have assured access to food will almost certainly lead to starvation and premature deaths.

Before rushing to condemn this government of inflicting violence on hapless and vulnerable citizens and of causing harm, we would do well to ponder why the government lapsed on its responsibilities. For instance, citizens living in region X may not get the food allotted to them because of poor administration, inadequate infrastructure, unseasonal rains which lead to losses of food stocks, corruption in the distribution of food, imperfect mapping of target populations, general insensitivity and cynicism, all those features of bad governance that Gupta elaborates so well. Irrespective of the exact combination of reasons why food has not been delivered, people have been harmed. This is indisputable.

Now consider a government that intentionally denies food to the poor in region Y, simply because it is inhabited by a religious or caste group that did not vote for the present government in the last election. The elected government decides to reward its supporters and penalize its opponents, even though it has announced a food-aid programme to help the poor, and a majority of the poor live in region Y.

Can we equate the two cases of failure to provide food? Surely not. In the first case, hunger and starvation is the outcome of a host of processes that might well belong to happenstance, for example a tornado might visit the region. Or, the government may be unable to extend help to people in need, because road robbers, or mercenaries or insurgents routinely hijack the convoy of trucks carrying food.

In the second case, the government decides not to provide food to citizens and *can* be held responsible for hunger-related deaths. In this case, harm has been caused by the intentional denial of basic rights of citizens. Let us not mistake the matter. Gupta is perfectly correct when he damns the Indian government for failing to implement its own programmes. Would he have not dammed the government in stronger terms if it had purposefully withheld anti-poverty programmes from militancy-hit areas such as Assam, Manipur, Chattisgarh and Kashmir?

Theorists of structural violence rule out intentionality as central to violence and responsible for harm. Harm is produced through a complex of processes that are difficult to unravel and moreover seem to be produced unintentionally. Consider now the implications of this formulation. Our roles in a society are produced and reproduced by violence and are predestined, or so it appears. We are fated to be either the vendors of or the addressees of violence. It depends on the social class we are born into. This practically rules out agency or the capacity to act according to our political judgement. Let alone act against the grain of our class dictates, we cannot, ever, be trapped in Hamlet's classic dilemma – to 'be' or not to 'be' violent.

There is more. If Ram intentionally injures Rati through acts of violence, he is morally responsible. We can allot moral responsibility for harm, only if we are convinced that Ram had set out deliberately to injure someone. Recollect that criminal law distinguishes between pre-mediated murder and extenuating circumstances such as diminished responsibility. If Ram has infringed the negative right of Rati not to be harmed, and in the process violated his own duty not to cause harm, he must be prepared to take responsibility for the act. This may range from imprisonment, to paying of compensation to the addressee of violence and/or her family, to community service. But if injury is caused unintentionally, or because Ram is the bearer of roles that structures have laid down for him, can we demand that he take on responsibility?

When it comes to the state and its personnel, the detachment of harm from intention and responsibility bears serious implications. State officials are practically liberated from complicity and thereby responsibility. And targets of violence have no one to fix blame on. They cannot, after all, demand redress or compensation from impersonal structures. Nor can they drag these structures to the bar from which justice is dispensed. The addresses of violence are, thereby, denied agency. Structural violence theories cannot really explain this aspect of human behaviour.

Speaking back to history

Recollect the upsurge against the state as well as dominant social groups in Tunisia, Egypt, Syria, Libya, Yemen, Bahrain, Saudi Arabia, Algeria, Morocco and other countries in the Middle East from December 2010 onwards. Protests that marked the 'Arab Spring' were sparked off when on 17 December 2010 a 26-year-old vegetable vendor Mohammed Bouazizi set himself on fire before a government building in the rural town of Sidi Bouzid in Tunisia. He committed self-immolation in protest against public humiliation heaped on him by a police officer. The act sparked off massive protests across the country and resulted in demands that President Zina El Abidina resign. A month later the president fled the country.

Notably, some countries that were rocked by protests were under military regimes, others under individual despots. The inhabitants of these societies had been denied basic rights such as freedom of expression and right to association. They had been harmed by unjust state structures. Yet people came together in crowded public places to protest against harm caused by definable acts, from abuse of authority, to upping bus fares in Brazil, to denial of rights. The protestors identified the perpetrators of injustice, demanded that they be punished for the injuries wreaked upon people and insisted on both retributive and remedial justice. What had been thought of as the unthinkable and improbable had been translated into the probable and the achievable. A number of successful autocrats were forced to demit office, Ben Ali in Tunisia, Hosni Mubarak in Egypt and Ali Abdullah Saleh in Yemen.

The Arab Spring might have fetched mixed results, significantly, however, civil societies in these countries have shown that they are able to stand up and speak back to histories not of their making and not to their liking. For many years, scholars had spoken of the resilience of authoritarianism in the Arab world and of dismal prospects of liberation. The adverse impact of neo-liberal reforms on the lives of people, combined with perceived lack of legitimacy of these regimes, culminated in massive protests, which took the government, the opposition and even civil society organizations by surprise. Notably in Egypt, the demand was not only for bread but also for freedom and human dignity.

Contesting violence

The proposition made by votaries of structural violence, that the state is nothing but a condensate of power and illegitimate violence, and that societies are governed by the relentless impulse to violence, or that violence runs rife, is frankly trite, outright banal. All states and all societies exhibit a relentless will to power. Our modern democratic state, backed as it is by weapons of mass destruction, is embedded in violence and engaged in a constant effort to subdue citizens. This is well known; it is even a given. But the modern democratic state also speaks the language of entitlements and rights, of representation and participation and of accountability and responsibility. Therefore, the state is, for many political groups, a field of expectations. It naturally becomes the target of collective protest when these expectations are betrayed. Protests against the state spill over into protests against symbolic or material power wielded by 'big men' in society. Where democracies have not been institutionalized, or where the army or dictators rule, the idea of democracy inspires people to fight for their right to liberty against the state and authoritarian societies. Where democracies have been inadequately institutionalized, protests demand the rollback of injustice and realization of the democratic idea.

Institutions of democracy often falter and falter seriously. This is particularly true of Indian democracy, which is, but, imperfectly realized. What is important is that the idea of democracy has inspired marginal groups to fight for what is right and what is their right both in state and in society. Some groups recover agency; some do not. But structural violence underplays crucial factors of intention, moral responsibility and agency. The concept cannot come to terms with the fact that yesterday's victims have today revealed enormous capacity both to speak back to histories not of their making and to make their own histories. These histories may not be the one they wanted to make in the first instance, but this is politically not all that significant. None of us make history in conditions of our own choice as Marx reminded us. What is important is that people want to make the transition from subject to citizen. It is this crucial factor of agency that often goes missing in theories of structural violence.

I do not mean to dismiss the concept of structural violence. It undeniably articulates the sense of frustration and anger at the high degree of tolerance society exhibits towards harm in general, and deprivation and exploitation in particular. But when we draw attention to these features, we *castigate* the kind of society we live in. We do not *conceptualize* violence. Arguably, theories of structural violence should be able to explain why I bear moral responsibility for something I did not do to another person who has been harmed, or if I did not intend that harm should be caused to another through my actions. This has to be explained and clarified. But it is precisely this theorists of structural violence do not explain.

If we need to know of what we speak when we speak of violence because we want to clarify processes that lead to political judgement, we should try not to extend the concept, overload it or using it as a handy synonym for other concepts. This route leads nowhere except to considerable conceptual muddles.

Discrete virtues of a parsimonious theory of violence

It is possible that the over-extension of a concept can lead to its implosion. For this reason, a coherent and a *political* concept of violence must necessarily be parsimonious (in the dictionary meaning of sparse or cheese-paring) *if* we want to know what we speak of when we speak of violence. For this, we need to distinguish the characteristics of violence and figure out which of these features *defines* violence.

The most obvious feature of violence is the use of force. In the English language, the etymological origin of violence can be traced to two terms of which the first is *violentus*. The term *violentus* captures the property of an act. For example, we could describe Rahim's act in shutting the door of his car with great force as violent. All that we mean to indicate is that Rahim shut the car door with more force than was required, or that he slammed the door shut by using excessive force. Here 'violent' is used purely descriptively. We can of course push the implication of the statement further and suggest that the act told us in graphic detail about the state of Rahim's mind. He was either furious or desperate, either frustrated or threatened or he might just have been in a hurry to keep an appointment because he was running late. What is incontrovertible is that the term 'violence' captures the dominant property of an act, or that it is used evocatively. Doors are opened and shut at fairly regular intervals and we hardly register this empirical fact. It is the insertion of 'violent' as a prefix to the act of shutting the car door that marks the act as worthy of note.

Note that as of now, Rahim's act in slamming the door shut with excessive force did not hurt anyone or infringe anyone's negative right not to be harmed. Matters are qualitatively different if his action injured Rehana, who exiting the car from the rear door had her hand on the doorjamb at the exact moment that Rahim slammed the door shut. The description of an act that harmed someone, because it was performed with more force than needed, as violence, corresponds to the word *violare* or violation of the right not to be harmed. This brings us to harm as the second component of violence. But, before we discuss harm, let us dwell on force a little more.

Force is, arguably, a generic feature of violent acts. Is force the *distinguishing* feature of violence? Perhaps not, for it is possible to distinguish between force and violence. Force can be used to protect someone. Rehana has to use some degree of force if she wants to prevent her child from running into a crowded road. Or, Rati might have to slap Rita, who is bent on committing suicide, hard so that the latter to her senses and reverses her decision to jump off the bridge into the angry, foaming sea. Rehana and Rati have used force, and the use of force causes injury. But it also prevents greater harm, an accident in the first case, and a suicide in the second. Second, in games such as soccer or boxing, the players use a great deal of force and often injure each other, but this can hardly be termed a case of violence as the deliberate infliction of harm. Descriptively we can describe these sports as violent. Third, actions can involve force but this does not harm anyone. Rahim, as we have seen, slammed a door shut with great force, but he did not harm anyone. Here again violence is used descriptively.

Conversely, people can be harmed without being subjected to excessive force. Think of sophisticated modes of torture that leave no trace on the corporeal body. Someone can be drugged before he is killed, or she can be put to death by administering highly sophisticated forms of poisoning that do not cause convulsions such as frothing at the mouth and savage biting of the tongue.

The strange story of the death of the Sphinx who guarded the doors of Thebes comes to mind in this context. Wandering through the land after he had visited the Oracle at Delphi, Oedipus confronts the Sphinx. This creature, half-human and half-animal, had been sent by the Gods to Thebes to punish the inhabitants for the sins committed by King Laius. Many moons ago, a soothsayer had warned Laius, the King of Thebes, and his wife, Jocasta, that their son would kill his father and marry his own mother and thus commit both incest and parricide.

A panic-stricken Laius ordered that the feet of his newly born son should be pierced and bound together, and that the baby should be abandoned on Mount Cithaeron to perish. Fate had a different future in store for the infant. Overcome by compassion, the servant handed over the infant to a shepherd who tended the sheep of King Polybus of Corinth. The baby, christened Oedipus because the injury to his ankles had led to swollen feet, was adopted by King Polybus and his Queen. In due course of time, Oedipus, rendered distraught by the rumour that he had been adopted, trekked to Delphi to consult the Oracle. Terrible news awaited him: that he was fated to kill his father and wed his mother. Determined to sidestep these twin scourges, Oedipus took the road away from Corinth. On the way, he entered into an altercation with a group of attendants carrying an elderly gentleman in a palanquin. During the ensuing scuffle, our benighted hero struck the elderly gentleman with his stick. The gentleman, who turned out to be King Laius, was killed on the spot. Completely oblivious to the fact that he had, after all, committed the grave sin of parricide exactly as a malevolent fate had ordained, Oedipus fled the spot. He subsequently came across the Sphinx who sat astride the gates of Thebes.

From this strategic perch, the Sphinx allowed people to enter into the city only if they could solve a riddle she posed to them. A dreadful fate awaited people who could not answer. They were devoured by the Sphinx, who had developed a taste for human flesh. The Sphinx, who had been anointed by the Gods to slowly but surely ruin Thebes, cut the city-state off from the rest of the world. Oedipus proved a saviour because, much to the astonishment of the Sphinx, he was able to solve the riddle. The Sphinx was so taken aback by his sharp intelligence that she threw herself off the cliff in either shock or utter desperation, or both. The fall put a violent end to the gatekeeper of Thebes. This must be the only case in history of a death brought on by a person, who in our world would be hailed as an expert at quizzing. In sum, the use of force may be used to prevent harm, it may not harm anyone and harm can be produced by factors other than force. Force is a component of violence, but it is not its defining feature.

Is then harm the constitutive aspect of violence? Despite major disagreements, theorists of violence generally accept that harm is central to the concept. But this is not the end of the story because harm can be caused intentionally or unintentionally. There is a finite difference between intentional and unintentional harm. To illustrate this point, let us revisit our earlier example. Rahim shut the car door with some force, and in the process, hurt Rehana whose hand was on the doorjamb. But Rahim might not have meant to hurt Rehana at all. He simply may not have noticed that the latter was also exiting the car. Can we seriously hold Rahim responsible for injuring his passenger? He acted thoughtlessly, we can conclude with some justification, and this thoughtlessness, or absent-mindedness or whatever his state of mind might have been at that time, caused distress.

Can we, in all honesty, blame him quite as much as we would have if he had shut the door on Rehana's hand intentionally, in full knowledge that she had placed her hand on the doorjamb? As suggested above, we cannot but acknowledge the difference between a government that fails to provide food to its citizens because trucks carrying food were hijacked and a government that intentionally holds back food from one section of citizens. In both cases, citizens suffer, but the moral responsibility of the government towards these citizens is surely greater in the second case than in the first. The distinction between knowing and not knowing, or intention and happenstance, has important implications for any judgement on violence.

This point is not of consequence to utilitarian philosophers who focus on harm and dispense with intentionality. Utilitarians insist that people are responsible not only for acts of commission, but also for those of omission, not only for what they did, but also for what they did not do. That is, they do not see any major difference between acts that cause harm and failure to perform an act, provided that we know that non-action will cause harm. Knowledge is in this case identified with intention.

The Marxist Utilitarian philosopher John Harris argues that deaths caused by indifference and neglect of society and its rulers must be seen as being as much as a part of violence as violent acts of revolutionaries. Why do we see a murder as a violent act, and not see that men can die because of starvation, neglect or abandonment? We assign moral responsibility to agents for acts of commission as well as omission, argues Harris, only if they intend to cause harm. They are equally responsible if they have done nothing to prevent harm. Within the conception of negative actions, Harris argues that people must be held responsible for not acting if they knew that they could prevent harm, and if they were in a position to do so.

The utilitarian argument, which attributes moral responsibility to both action and non-action, is both powerful and deeply disturbing. Someone somewhere has caused harm, and that person must accept moral responsibility and make amends. The implications are, however, troublesome. Every time I fail to contribute to a charity that I know provides poor children education, food or literacy or healing, I perform an act of violence. But surely there is a qualitative difference between not contributing to a charity because I forgot and injuring someone directly by knifing her.

If I set out to injure, say, Rati, I am culpable and therefore morally responsible. Will I be culpable if I fail to save Rati from harm? Certainly failure to avert harm is morally condemnable. If I watch someone assaulting Rati and do not intervene, I am, rightly speaking a coward. Does cowardice imply that I am *responsible* for Rati's injuries? Negligence and cowardice are morally significant in so far as they are undesirable attributes of the human condition, but surely intentionality is even more significant to morality. Intention is central to violence.

The belief that intention defines violence presumes voluntary action in so far as I had a choice between doing and not doing harm. I, or you, the state or non-state actor, chose to do harm, and this makes each of us morally responsible. Consider, for instance, the distinction between two sorts of acts. A car driver causes an accident and injures people, not intentionally but because he had a cardiac attack while at the wheel. Compare this incident with the case of a car driver who under the influence of alcohol runs over people sleeping on the pavements of Delhi. Who is morally culpable and responsible, and who should compensate the victims of violence, the person who had no choice or someone who had a choice and chose badly? Intention is central to violence and is a defining feature of violence. More significantly, intention carries the factor of moral responsibility. It is the factor of choice that distinguishes the concept of violence from descriptions of an act as violent, because it allows us to make judgements.

What does the discussion above tell us? An act that involves a considerable degree of force or energy can certainly be described as violent, but it need not establish a social relation between persons. Second, a social relationship can be established through the use of force and the infliction of harm. But if the use of force is not intentional, the person who has inflicted harm unintentionally may not be considered morally responsible. Third, the intentional use of force to cause harm is central to the concept of violence. Intention makes the person who performs a violent act morally responsible. This is a basic code of justice. While driving if I take a right turn without indicating that I am doing so and cause an accident, I am responsible and must compensate the victim. But if a car hits me while my car is stationary at a traffic light, I cannot be blamed. The other driver has caused an accident. In both cases, harm was caused, but the allotment of moral responsibility takes different roads.

Let me wrap up the argument above. Central to the concept of violence is intention. This naturally excludes natural disasters that cause massive harm from the conceptual category of violence. A storm that wrecks everything in its path leads to immense harm. People are uprooted, dislocated, and killed, property destroyed and the environment devastated. Storms or 'acts of God' cause harm, but can we place this incident within the conceptual category of violence? Properly we cannot, because in this case, we can neither discover a purposeful agent nor an identifiable victim whom our agent intends to harm. Harm has been caused, and *descriptively* the storm that caused harm can certainly be termed violent.

Conceptually, matters are different because violence does not belong to happenstance, or something that is an unintended by-product of processes independent of human volition, or something that is, because it cannot be otherwise. Intention implies that an agent, whether a non-state actor, or the state or both, choose to inflict violence on others. If they chose to inflict violence, they must bear responsibility for these acts, be punished and/or be forced to compensate for harm. It is this dimension of violence that has gone missing in theories of structural violence.

And now for some conceptual muddles

Structural or systemic violence is a flexible concept that seeks to explain everything from babies dying of diarrhoea in poverty-stricken areas of India, to acts of terror committed by agents at war with a particular religion or an ideology. Refusing to accept intention as central to the concept, votaries of this avatar seek to immerse every social evil in the vocabulary of violence. Take Gupta's suggestion that persons who benefit from the system participate, unwittingly no doubt, in violence against those who do not benefit. There is room for puzzlement. People can be and are insensitive to the poor who inhabit the same society, and who are metaphorically speaking their neighbours. They can rightfully be categorized as indifferent, callous, selfish and blameworthy, but violent? The mind boggles. The problem should be clear by now. Because the concept of violence has been subjected to indiscriminate expansion, it has become a stand-in concept, or an easy synonym for other concepts that can arguably capture processes that cause harm, to more effect.

In any case, what, we can rightfully wonder, is the specific advantage of using violence as a stand-in category for other concepts that also relate to ill-being? We have a range of concepts at hand, such as oppression, discrimination, social injustice and exploitation that both capture and describe specific forms of ill-being. All these concepts inform us that certain wrongs have been done to human beings, and that these should not have been done.

Note, however, that the processes that lead to wrongdoing, or to harm, are fairly distinctive, even if they overlap. Consider discrimination. The concept of discrimination tells us that a group of people have been denied benefits such as the right to life and liberty, freedom of expression and association; the right to form trade unions; and the right to health care, education, employment or income that are readily available to other members of society, for reasons that are purely arbitrary, belonging to the 'wrong' ethnic group for instance. If I am denied the right to freedom of expression, movement and assembly merely because I live in a region that is marked by insurgency, I am *discriminated* against. Discrimination takes place when we are denied what others in our society are entitled to, for no justified reason. The imposition of draconian acts such as the Armed Forces Special Powers Act, which grant immunity to army personnel during the course of their duty in the Kashmir Valley and in the North-East of India, amounts to rank discrimination. The inhabitants of these regions suffer from infirmities that other Indians do not for no fault of their own, they are, therefore, discriminated against.

If the owner of a textile unit makes his workers labour for long hours without adequate remuneration, this particular form of injustice is properly called exploitation. If I am denied an equal share in the benefits that my society has to offer, and if I have to bear a disproportionate share of the burdens of this society, I am the victim of social injustice.

When millions of Scheduled Castes and Scheduled Tribes in poverty-stricken areas in central and east India suffer from avoidable harm, eke out a bare existence, continue to be subjected to rank indignities and die premature deaths, their situation is best conceptualized as social injustice. When the security forces of the state fire upon them without any justification, and when this leads to injuries and death, this is best conceptualized as violence. When a particular group bears a disproportionate share of the burden of a society, without participating in the benefits that society has to offer, we properly term this a case of social injustice. Violence occurs when we are physically harmed. Violence and injustice are wrong in different ways. Violence infringes our right to bodily integrity; injustice denies people a fair share in the benefits and instead puts the burdens on their shoulders. Both harm but in distinctive ways.

In this precise context, Vittorio Buffachi makes an interesting argument. He suggests that if we make an equation between violence and injustice, the course of argument is simplistic, misleading and reductionist. If a theory of justice is to eradicate injustice, then we must understand exactly why injustice is bad and wrong. This is where the literature on violence can help us. A comprehensive study of the concept of violence can help us to make sense of the meaning of injustice, as well as engender a more extensive commitment to social justice as the only antidote against violence. What appears nebulous in terms of injustice becomes much clearer in terms of violence. We cannot understand injustice, suggests Buffachi, simply by calling it another name, viz injustice. But when we inverse the roles, start from a theory of violence, and analyse injustice in terms of violence, we realize that injustice is bad and wrong for the same reasons that violence is bad and wrong. The reason is that both victims of injustice and violence are humiliated and feel powerless and vulnerable.[6] I think Buffachi makes a valuable contribution to the understanding of both injustice and violence. Whereas he makes a distinction between the two concepts, he suggests that the impact of injustice on the victim is similar to impact of violence on the same or other victims. In other words, he explores the concept of injustice through the prism of the concept of violence.

Let me take the argument on the distinctiveness of concepts made by Buffachi further. The fact that two distinct processes breed the same kind of consequences does not warrant the conclusion that these two processes can be collapsed into each other. An inspiring piece of music enchants, watching a skilful cricketer play excites and a beautifully written book produces pleasure and exhilaration. Delight, excitement, pleasure and exhilaration are companion emotions in so far as they promote a sense of happiness. But by that fact alone, we cannot assume that a game of cricket is akin to an inspiring piece of music or to a piece of wonderfully and elegantly written prose. Similarly, whereas it is true that violence harms and harms abundantly, injustice harms equally abundantly. Just because the consequences that follow both violence and injustice are similar, that is, harm and injury, why should we proceed to substitute one term for another? Buffachi makes the same point from a different vantage point.

Moreover, when theorists bring different kinds of social and political concepts under the umbrella of violence, they simply do not recognize that different strategies are at hand to remedy the wrong inflicted upon human beings. Suppose Rati is a victim of domestic violence, and she appeals to a women's group for help. By now, women's groups more or less know how to deal with domestic violence: drag the erring spouse to court under the Protection of Women from Domestic Violence Act 2005. But if Rati's interests have been harmed because she has been denied her rightful share in parental property, a different sort of process is at work; that of skewed property rights in a patriarchal society that is unjust to women. In this case, feminists will have to invoke the Hindu Succession Amendment Act 2005, to help her fight for her legitimate right.

In the first case, Rati has been subjected to excessive physical force, and this has infringed her negative right not to be harmed. The consequences of this infringement are serious: wounds, fractured bones, torn ligaments, bruises, scars, a shattered psyche and ruined confidence. In the second case of denial of equal property rights, her psyche will certainly be in tatters because she realizes that as a daughter she does not count as an equal with her male siblings. But this is the outcome of gender injustice, not of the use of excessive force that infringes her basic rights.

Certainly, violence as part of political rhetoric plays a powerful role in arousing moral outrage, but we might fail to understand what is so distinctive about particular ways of causing harm. There is arguably a substantive distinction between being denied social and economic rights, and unmarked graves, encounter deaths, mutilation, rape, stabbings, strangulation, decapitating, burning and drowning. The concept of violence is best reserved for the latter category of cases. Why should we carry out this substitution in any case? In a democracy, injustice is as much a cause for anger, resentment and protest, as violence. If we use the two concepts as synonyms, not only are our political vocabularies reduced and we become alarmingly monolingual, we can no longer distinguish between the ills of the human condition, the causes of these ills or indeed the remedies for these maladies.

Conclusion

Till now the argument has sought to establish that we need to know of what we speak when we speak of violence. The concept of violence needs to be clarified simply because it has been subjected to a great deal of overuse, mainly because it is a high-impact word. In order to be clear what we speak of when we speak of violence, this argument has tried to clarify the concept by putting forth a parsimonious concept of violence. First, violence is a social act in so far as it establishes a relationship of power and domination between two or more persons. An act that deploys considerable force, such as an act of slamming a door shut, can be *described* as violent, but it has not harmed anyone, and thereby has not established a social relation. Second, violence generally, but not always, involves a degree of force. It is possible to intentionally harm other persons through means other than force, administering sophisticated poison to the unhappy target for instance. Third, acts of violence can cause harm, but we must remember that harm can be caused by other factors that do not involve the use of force. Fourth, any definition that allows us to make informed judgements on acts of violence sees intention, and therefore culpability and responsibility as central to the concept. Fifth, a parsimonious definition helps us understand the distinction between violence and other wrongs such as social injustice or discrimination. Parsimonious conceptions of violence help us to comprehend the distinctiveness of political and more specifically revolutionary violence, which involves determinate agents, intention, use of force, harm and moral responsibility.

The Saga of Revolutionary Violence in India

Introduction

A parsimonious definition of violence enables us to understand the distinctiveness of political violence, as intentional acts that involve coercion and force and lead to harm. More importantly, this genre of violence is targeted towards effecting changes in the state and in its policies. Revolutionary violence is distinct from other form of political violence in so far as revolutionaries deny the legitimacy of the state, seek the overthrow of state power through armed struggle and attempt to put in place a state that is less unjust than the one we live in at present. The state tries to suppress or, at least, contain the armed struggle through all the means at its command: imposition of draconian legislation, suspension of civil liberties, torture of suspects, relocation of villagers, destruction of Maoist hideouts and indiscriminate killings.

State violence causes harm on an unprecedented scale. Revolutionary violence causes harm on an unprecedented scale. Caught between the state and revolutionaries are innocent people, oft the very people on whose behalf the gun was picked up in the first place, as well as officials who are in the business of performing their allotted roles. In this section, I chart out a brief biography of Maoism in India, to highlight this very point.

The outbreak of revolutionary violence in India

In India, the saga of revolutionary violence that was initiated in 1967 sent tremors of shock and awe through the country and abroad. In some quarters, both domestic and international, the armed uprising was enthusiastically hailed. On 5 July 1967, an editorial in the *People's Daily*, the official newspaper of the Chinese Communist Party, triumphantly proclaimed that 'A peal of spring thunder has crashed over the land of India'. The reference was to a peasant uprising in the Naxalbari area in Darjeeling district in March of that year, when sharecroppers and landless labour, raising the slogan of 'land to the tiller' revolted against local landlords. The editorial went on to predict that 'a great storm of revolutionary armed struggle will eventually sweep over the length and the breadth of India'. In a fairly short time, what came to be known as the Naxalbari uprising spread over parts of West Bengal and spilled over into Andhra Pradesh, Orissa, Bihar, Madhya Pradesh, Uttar Pradesh, Punjab and Kerala. Some of these states, or rather regions within these states, continue to be wracked by armed struggle waged by Maoist guerrillas.

A number of observers have traced the armed uprising to the deep ideological divide in the international communist movement of the time. Relations between the communist parties of the Soviet Union and the Peoples' Republic of China had soured on the twin issue of strategy and objectives. The hail of epithets hurled by one side of the divide at the other, ranged from 'left-wing adventurism' (for the CPC) to the dreaded term 'revisionist' (for the CPSU), escalated into a diplomatic crisis and ruptured relations between the two countries. In 1969, the two armies were to clash on the border between the Soviet Union and China.

The deep divide in the international communist movement led to a split in the Communist Party in India (CPI) in 1964 and generated a second left formation, the Communist Party Marxist (CPIM). Despite superficial divisions on the political line, each party wanted to pursue: the one established by the CPSU, or the one mandated by the CPC, both parties remained committed to the electoral route to parliamentary democracy and to the paraphernalia that comes along with competitive party politics. In a short span of time, another split within the CPIM generated a third communist formation.

The split was catalysed by a group led by Charu Majumdar, who had challenged the leadership on every front, from its analysis of Indian society to the strategy it espoused for dealing with the manifold problems of an impoverished peasantry. In a series of eight essays published between 1965 and 1967, Majumdar attacked the CPIM for rescinding on Maoist ideology and for opting for a strategy that was practically irrelevant to the needs of Indian society. Following the Maoist line, the breakaway faction declared that the chief contradiction in a semi-feudal and semi-colonial India is between the peasantry and the landlords. This seemingly irreconcilable divide can be resolved, it was declared, only through armed struggle, the overthrow of the state and the establishment of a People's Democracy. Power, Charu Majumdar insisted, following to the last alphabet the signature script of Mao Ze Dong, flows from the barrel of the gun. Expectedly, Majumdar was expelled from the CPIM in 1967.

Charu Majumdar had cut his teeth on revolutionary politics when he took part in a violent peasant uprising in 1946 in Bengal. The Tebhaga uprising was firmly anchored in the demand for redistributive justice, more specifically in the claim that the share of the landlord in the produce should be reduced from a half to one-third. Spearheaded by a rising Communist Party of India, Tebhaga catapulted an issue of crucial significance onto the political agenda, the right of the worker over the product of her labour. The entrenched power of the landlord over the bodies and the labour of the peasant was sought to be ruptured through violent clashes and looting of granaries. The movement was repressed and collapsed, but it left a legacy that was to inspire other peasant movements against exploitative landlords, usurious moneylenders and corrupt forest and revenue officials.

One such movement took place in West Bengal. In the 1950s, communist activists led by Kanu Sanyal and Khokhan Majumdar had begun to organize peasants and workers into Kisan Sabhas in the Jalpaiguri district of Bengal. Charu Majumdar and Jangal Santhal joined the movement a little later and began to mobilize landless labour, sharecroppers, small peasants and tea-garden workers to confront the untrammelled power of landowners and carry out redistribution of appropriated land.

Political mobilization bore fruit and armed struggle broke out in Naxalbari, Phansidewa and Kharibari villages in 1967. Landless workers, sharecroppers, small peasants, and tea-garden workers rose in revolt on the plank of land to the tiller. Naxalbari, which lies in the Terai region of Darjeeling district, was known for tea plantations established by British and Indian companies. Labour from the tribal areas of Jharkand and Madhya Pradesh had been rounded up to work in these large tea gardens which had been exempted from the scope of land reform legislation and ceiling acts implemented by the Government of India shortly after independence. It was this region that became the epicentre of the armed uprising that popularly came to be known as Naxalbari.

It is a moot point that practically every decade of post-independence India has been wracked by some crisis or the other. In retrospect, the decade of the 1960s proved especially momentous. All hopes that the post-independence political elite had, either the inclination or the will, to implement promises made by the first-generation leadership of independent India dramatically collapsed. The post-colonial elite had failed to live up to its own commitments, the Congress party which had led the mass movement against colonialism degenerated into a party of courtiers striving for proximity to the leader, the left had been tamed by the exigencies of parliamentary politics and millions of Indians continued to suffer from conceivably every ill of the human condition. In 1947, the great poet Faiz Ahmad Faiz had written the obituary of independence, the other side of which was the partition of the country. 'This stained dawn, this shadowed morn, this is not the morn we struggled for', he wrote in utmost desolation. The anguish epitomized in the poem was a damming indictment of partition politics. Twenty years later he could have written the same stanza as an epitaph, mourning the failure of the post-colonial elite to deliver justice to its own people in country after country in the post-colonial world.

Amidst this rampant discontent and generalized hopelessness, an ideologically grounded armed struggle of the dispossessed and the rural poor took on the might of the Indian state. It is not as if tribals, the landless and the small peasant had not revolted against injustice in India earlier. In 1967, these isolated and often random outbursts of violence were consolidated and strengthened by the ideology and strategy of guerrilla war fashioned by Mao Ze Dong. The strategy and the vision of Mao had been vindicated by the victory of the Chinese Communist Party in 1949 and the defeat of French forces by the Vietnamese at Dien Bien Phu in 1954.

Majorly inspired by Maoism, Naxalism presented to the youth a new political imaginary, that of a society free of exploitation and injustice in which the self could fashion itself in freedom from social, economic and political constraints. As news about the peasant uprising spread to towns and cities, young people, deeply disillusioned by hopes belied and optimism betrayed, were charged with new sense of excitement and anticipation. Students, belonging to elite schools and universities, and professionals, in rewarding jobs, left their privileged niches and joined the Naxalite movement in various parts of the country. Posters supporting Naxalbari and Chairman Mao were pasted on the walls of buildings and parks in Calcutta and, in particular, in College Street. On the lawns of the elite Presidency College, famous for having produced intellectuals of extraordinary merit and ability, students from the college and elsewhere congregated to discuss violent revolution, a theme that was till then confined to the pages of the spectacularly written *The Wretched of the Earth* and to tales of revolutionary movements in rural areas of Vietnam and China. In St Stephens College in Delhi University, one of the premier colleges in the country, slogans acclaiming the important role of Chairman Mao in shaping revolutionary imaginaries blazoned from the main tower.

Fired by the hope that India could replicate revolutionary peasant rebellions in other developing countries, students joined the exodus to the rural areas. Fairly soon however, a section of the youth that had left families, universities and well-paid jobs came to be disillusioned with the call to annihilate class enemies and with Charu Majumdar's injunction that their hands should be stained with the blood of the class enemy. The ritual of bloodletting marked the transition from the pre-revolutionary to the revolutionary. Staining of one's hands with the blood of others was nothing short than a rite of passage, baptism into politics in the revolutionary mode.

To date, Charu Majumdar is slammed for his insistence that the annihilation of class enemies is a higher form of class struggle and for his emphasis on the need to physically liquidate feudal classes in the countryside, along with landowners, moneylenders and other agents of a semi-feudal and semi-colonial society. This many could not stomach. The gifted director Sudhir Mishra in his 2003 film *Hazaron Khawaishen Aisi* forcefully captured the dilemma of students belonging to the elite strata of society, trapped between the requirement to commit violent acts and police torture if they did so, or even if they did not do so. Some opted out of the struggle, left for foreign universities and became established academics, others joined the civil service and yet others the corporate sector.

But others stayed behind to fight. Red Guard squads formed in schools and colleges served as a precursor of the People's Liberation Army. The period of discontent saw quixotic revolutionaries instigating workers to rise against capitalists, denouncement of class enemies, desecration of statues of revered leaders, raids on government offices, gheraos, strikes, attacks on police personnel and damage to public property. In rural areas, peasant militias armed often with only bows and arrows seized grain from the kulaks. The escalation of violence led to deaths in police firing, abduction and killing of landlords and snatching of arms.

In retrospect, the revolution was premature and definitely more romantic than revolutionary in its programme and its objectives. Manoranjan Mohanty argues that the movement was pre-organizational, it mechanically applied formulations of the Chinese revolution in India and that it concentrated more on violence and less on politicization of the constituency it spoke on behalf of.[1] More significantly, the struggle sparked off state repression and catapulted the expansion of paramilitary forces. Thus was the rather sad epigraph of a movement, which strongly gripped the political imagination of many a young person fired by the ambition to liberate India from the ills the post-independence leadership had consigned the country to, written.

The global context

Discontent with the establishment was not confined to the youth in India. Revolutionary romanticism and a passionate desire for a new order that could deliver justice and eliminate injustice exploded across the globe at the decade of the 1970s, firing minds and sparking off imaginations. Campus revolts broke out in the 1960s in the US, Germany, France, Italy, Japan, Mexico and other countries of the west. Young people rejected the ideas, the institutions and the visions of a liberal capitalist order that had been forged in the aftermath of the Second World War. In France, in May/June 1968, a crisis of unprecedented magnitude overpowered the country as students revolted against poor educational conditions and authoritarian administrations. Young people demanded free access to universities and more personal and political freedoms, and workers demanded power. The police crackdown resulted in injuries and arrests of scores of students. Demonstrations in Paris and other cities against police brutality swelled, and a general strike paralysed the country as labour joined students in solidarity. In May 1968, 10 million French workers went on strike and occupied factories. The French government headed by Charles de Gaulle was forced to capitulate and resign.

In the United States, campus revolts against US involvement in the Vietnam War articulated a generalized ethos of rebellion against the established order. The civil liberties movements, gender struggles for equality, the struggle for the right to sexual preferences and rebellions in ghettos of American cities dissipated expectations that the American way of life would provide a luminous model for the rest of the world to follow. Hundreds of thousands of Afro-Americans participating in urban protests mounted a formidable challenge to practices of discrimination and racism, as well as poor housing, dismal schooling, unemployment and police brutality.

Revolts and popular discontent across the world challenged the precepts of not only liberal democracy and the market order, but also statist communism that had been institutionalized in the Soviet Union. The old Soviet style left was denounced and dismissed as moribund, as unable to offer any solution whatsoever, and indeed as part of the problem. It was Mao with his emphasis on the autonomy of politics who became the inspiration for youth in rebellion.

Many of these protests, opting as they did for piecemeal strategies of violence, and lacking as they did sustained leadership and a coherent and focussed ideology, quickly dissipated or were sternly repressed. In India, the state cracked down on the Naxalites in West Bengal. The Indian army and the police launched project 'Operation Steeplechase' and constructed an outer corridor to cordon off areas affected by the uprising in Bengal, Bihar and Orissa. The paramilitary force, the Central Reserve Police Force rapidly mopped up cadres of the political formation within the enclosure.

The idea of revolution in post-independence India had spread like the proverbial bushfire across the country, but the revolution itself lasted not too long, hardly fifty-two days. Within two years, the armed struggle in West Bengal and in Andhra Pradesh where it had spread was suppressed ruthlessly by the state. Top leaders and cadres were detained, tortured and killed. Charu Majumdar was arrested on 16 July 1972 and died twelve days later in police custody. The police did not hand over his body to his family, and he was given a quiet burial. His comrade Jangal Santhal turned into an alcoholic and headed towards a disgraceful end in 1981. Kanu Sanyal was to disown violence and opt for parliamentary democracy. In 2010 he committed suicide.

The legacy of Naxalism

With the benefit of hindsight, what are we to make of the Naxalite revolt against institutionalized injustice inflicted upon the tribals and the dalits, and its wider objective of taking over state power? For the Naxalite leadership, a semi-feudal, semi-colonial order had been constructed upon the backs of an exploited peasantry. There was no alternative but the demolition of the old order and the establishment of a new one. The cadres of the party could help the peasants to secure some redress for immediate problems, through violent appropriation of land for instance. But the fuller realization of justice had to await a new order. It was a project for the future, and it was precisely this project that the Indian state was determined to extinguish.

Classical Marxist theories of revolution emphasize not only the role of the vanguard party in developing revolutionary consciousness among the people, but also objective conditions such as an economic crisis of great magnitude and a pervasive crisis of state legitimacy. The Maoists focussed on the subjective dimension; that is the primacy of politics, without gauging accurately the strengths of the democratic state in India. Nor did they think of linking up with other radical struggles, for example trade union and peasant movement, or movements of the tribals. The Naxalites waged an isolated war, and they continue to do so to date, despite all the rhetoric about forming coalitions with struggles of the dispossessed.

Allegations of adventurism, of fostering of an ill thought-out experiment, of fomenting a culture of bloodlust, of reducing ideology to dogma and of giving preference to polemics over argument continue to be made against the Naxalite movement. But, it would also be foolhardy to denounce Naxalism as so much hyper-adventurism. The Naxalites did not achieve their end: that of smashing state power or even the power of local power elites that held tribals and landless peasants in their deadly thrall. What Naxalism did was to catapult into the limelight the complete failure of the Indian government to look after the interests and the needs of the most vulnerable and those who are at risk. The Naxals spoke for those who lacked voice in Indian politics, gave them voice and focussed upon dispossession, exploitation and injustice. Voices from the margins resounded in the public sphere of politics, simply because peasants had reached for the gun or backed gun-holders who spoke for them. For the dispossessed, violence was the weapon of the last resort; the ideology of the triply disadvantaged, and the ultimate mode of protest politics.

Naxalbari failed, but it highlighted the urgent need to complete the unfinished business of securing the livelihood of the most marginal of the Indian people. Ironically, it was the armed revolt that compelled the state to take urgent cognizance of the dismal conditions in which tribals and poor dalit peasants lived out what passed for a life. Today, the region of Naxalbari has seen economic development. It is far removed from the poverty-stricken areas in which a group of armed revolutionaries had sought to wage a guerrilla struggle against the post-colonial state that had failed on all fronts, especially that of social justice, or of securing to all citizens basic rights, dignity, freedom, equality and justice, in short all the staples of our constitutional morality. Ironically, the economic development of the region also inaugurated the end of the revolutionary imaginary in the very space in which it had taken birth and acquired shape. The movement died out in the area where it had originated.

Post-Naxalbari

Remarkably, the defeat of the Naxalite movement did not herald the end of the story. The armed struggle had collapsed in Naxalbari, but the *idea* of Naxalbari continued to inspire those who fight for the dispossessed. In the late 1960s and early 1970s, bases for radical armed struggle were created in the hills and forests of the country in Andhra Pradesh, Orissa, Bihar and in West Bengal. Regions which saw the eruption of armed struggle are today part of Naxal folklore. Leaders who spoke for the marginalized have become symbols of a politics of the impossible, giants who carried the fight for a more just society on their shoulders. Under the protection of armed Naxal groups, peasants seized land that had been unjustly appropriated from them and harvested the produce. Poor and landless peasants led by guerrilla squads drove out landlords from villages, set up liberated zones and established people's courts to redistribute land and mete out justice through annihilation of class enemies.

But the struggle was not only about material gain. Tribals and dalits rose in a massive struggle for dignity that had been denied to them by inhuman caste practices and for control over means of subsistence that had been appropriated through exploitation, fraud and violence not only by upper but also by the intermediate castes. The latter had benefited from the limited land reforms that had been implemented, for the most part half-heartedly and reluctantly, in parts of India.

Some of these struggles have gone down in history as turning points in our collective life. When people who have been socially and economically dominated and exploited stand up and speak back to those who have taken away their land and the product of their labour, stripped them of their self-respect and denied them the status due to human beings, we see the enlargement of the political space. We witness the awesome phenomenon of the voiceless acquiring agency and speaking back to history. The method by which they acquire political agency, violence, might not meet with our approval, but that they acquire political agency is itself remarkable in our accursed caste-ridden, exclusionary and hierarchical society.

Yet, the story of Naxalism post-Naxalbari was not only one of giving to the dispossessed agency. The second phase of the Naxal struggle was marked by a great deal of fragmentation along personal rather than ideological lines, with groups professing copyright over the ideology, the strategy and the objectives of Naxalism, and locked into deadly battles with each other. The phase was marked by the degeneration of the revolutionary struggle, and consequent descent into mindless acts of violence. Immense violence scarred not only the bodies of landlords, but also those of small farmers, petty government employees, members of rival political parties and anyone suspected of being a police informer, including former comrades who had dissented from the line of the Naxal leadership.

Sumanta Bannerjee concludes that the history of the last four decades of the Naxalite movement in India is a painful record of attempts, both heroic and loutish, to bring about revolutionary changes in the benighted economic and social living conditions of the poor. Courageous battles against vicious state machinery, followed by self-sacrifice by thousands of guerrillas, and patient efforts by dedicated cadres to initiate land reform, and bring about changes in their areas of control, were marred by lumpen acts of extortions from petty traders and contractors and ruthless killings of people suspected to be police informers. The second phase in effect saw both the degeneration of revolutionary ideology and the fragmentation of the movement.[2]

The third phase

In September 2004, a new and a qualitatively different phase of the Maoist armed struggle, distinguished both by a transformation of the agent and of the political and economic context, was sparked off by the unification of two of the most significant groups in the movement. The first group, Peoples War, was the outcome of the 1998 merger between Peoples War Group and CPI (ML) Party Unity (PU). The second component, the Maoist Communist Centre, had formed an alliance with Revolutionary Communist Centre of India-Maoists in 2003. The upshot of the merger was the constitution of the Communist Party of India (Maoist).

The armed wings of the two groups merged and generated the Peoples Liberation Guerrilla Army. According to reports, membership of the armed militia of the Maoists ranges from 9,000 to 10,000 armed fighters. The militia has the backing of about 40,000 full-time cadres of the party. A majority of these are in the Bastar region alone. The PLGA reportedly possesses sophisticated weapons such as rocket launchers, AK 47s rifles, grenades and land mines. Notably, the leadership of the Maoists is non-tribal hailing mainly from Bihar and Andhra Pradesh. This raises, as we shall see, an important political issue that is taken up later in this work, in chapter five, the relationship between cadres of the party and the constituency on whose behalf arms have been raised.

The stated objective of the formation of the CPI Maoist, an event that was publicized through rallies, public meetings and the Internet, is to take over state power through armed struggle. The armed struggle or the people's democratic revolution and a peoples' democracy will function in the interests of the poor. This is textbook Maoism, familiar not only to those who follow Mao or condemn him and his ideology, but also to all newspaper readers. What is more interesting is the reason given for the guerrilla war, and the manner in which the Maoist leadership justifies armed struggle.

Renouncing the parliamentary path to democracy, a form of government that has been dismissed as corrupt and as corrupting, the party has declared war on the Indian state. There is in Maoist ideology no other way to establish peoples power. Neither elections, nor participation, neither representation, nor accountability of the rulers to the ruled will do. Faithful to the strategy of guerrilla war, the leadership holds that liberated zones in the rural hinterland have to be expanded to encircle the cities and overwhelm them.

The objectives of the Maoists are in the main two. The first objective is to launch a struggle in regions that experience extreme deprivation. The second objective is to overthrow the state in India and establish a people's democracy through armed struggle. Towards this end, the party cadres have been assigned the task of explaining to constituencies the need for enormous sacrifices, particularly since the army has launched an all-out offensive. The cadres are expected to initiate measures to unite with other struggling organizations and forces, to forge strong united fronts in various parts of the country and to gain the support of the masses in fighting and defeating superior enemy forces. Notably, the agent of revolutionary struggle has been transformed in so far as we see the consolidation of hitherto disparate forces, and the formation of an impressive political formation determined to defy the might of the Indian state.

The context of the new phase of Maoism has also been transformed. In order to understand the scale of this transformation, let us briefly visit some regions in the Maoist heartland. These can best be characterized in John Bunyan's words as a veritable 'slough of despond'. Here little babies die of malnutrition and preventable diseases like dysentery and malaria; women suffer from life-threatening diseases such as anaemia and malnutrition; poverty relentlessly stalks lives of people; and disease, illiteracy and hunger are their constant companions. It is precisely these regions that the Maoists have made their base. Newer forms of exploitation in the form of leasing or sale of resource rich land to private companies have worsened the situation.

Contextualizing revolutionary violence

Disagreements on how many Indians belong to the category of the absolute poor is an enduring and even a constitutive aspect of the Great Indian Poverty Debate. The debate structured in the main around methodological disputes on how to measure poverty and the poor has acquired highly technical overtones, and most of these subtleties escape non-economists, or more precisely non-statisticians. But even a non-economist can figure out that there is something very specific about poverty in India.

The Institute of Applied Manpower Research of the Planning Commission, Government of India, has constructed a state-wise Human Development Index. The index is based on three indices, health (life expectancy at birth), education (adjusted mean years of schooling and literacy rate for population aged 7 years and above) and income (standard of living determined by people's command over resources necessary to access food, shelter and clothing).[3] On the basis of these indices, the Human Development Report issued by the Institute has graded states in India. Poverty, according to the report, is concentrated in eight states in the central and the eastern parts of the country: Bihar, Chattisgarh, Jharkand, Madhya Pradesh, Odisha, Rajasthan and West Bengal, along with some parts of Uttar Pradesh. These states, with the exception of West Bengal, have been at the bottom of human development ranking list since 1999–2000. A majority of these states form part of the 'Red Corridor', which is marked by armed struggle.

More significantly, poverty is concentrated in mainly two communities: the Scheduled Tribes and the Scheduled Castes, and some groups in the Backward Castes. The 2010 UNDP Human Development Report affirms that 81 per cent of the STs, 66 per cent of the SCs and 58 per cent of OBCs belong to the category of multi-dimensionally poor.[4] (I concentrate on the plight of the SC and the ST population in these regions, because they suffer from double disadvantage, that of material deprivation as well as social discrimination.)

According to the latest statistics issued by the Institute of Applied Manpower Research, 48 per cent of all the Scheduled Castes and 52 per cent of the Scheduled Tribe population of the entire country lives in Bihar, Chattisgarh, Jharkand, Madhya Pradesh, Odisha, Rajasthan, Uttar Pradesh and Uttarakhand. A break-up of HDI statistics state wise presents a starker picture of the overlap between poor regions and poverty/low human development indicators among SC and ST communities. Chattisgarh, Bihar, Madhya Pradesh, Jharkand and Odisha are the worst performers on this front.

The overlap between absolute poverty and birth into a community that occupies a lowly position in the caste hierarchy is not happenstance. People are not poor because they lack basic skills to participate in profitable transactions; they are poor because they have been born into a community that has been historically stigmatized by the caste system as the (former) 'untouchable', the 'polluting' or the 'outsider'. Children born into these two social categories have been for centuries handed down nothing but deprivation, social discrimination, rank indignities and performance of menial tasks as their patrimony. Thomas Gray's (1716–1771) haunting and poignant words on penury in his 'Elegy written in a Country Churchyard' sums up the life many Indians are forced to lead in regions of eastern and central India. 'Perhaps in this neglected spot is laid some heart once pregnant with celestial fire/ Hands that the rod of empire might have swayed, or worked to ecstasy the living lyre/But Knowledge to their eyes her ample page/Rich with the spoils of time did ne'er unroll/Chill penury repress'd their noble rage/And froze the genial current of the soul'.

The link that the Indian state has tried to forge between group representation, redistribution and recognition through affirmative action policies has proved tenuous, and whatever benefits these policies have fetched are unevenly distributed. Both redistribution and recognition continue to elude persons in the poorest regions that have now been overrun by the Maoists. If we look at the regions in which the armed guerrilla squads of the Maoists operate, these dovetail neatly into areas in which the poorest of the poor and the most deprived of the doubly disadvantaged live and work.

The eminent author Mahashweta Devi, known for her evocative and powerful prose, her political commitment to marginal tribal communities in West Bengal and Jharkand and her castigation of various processes that create and recreate dispossession and homelessness in India, has sternly reprimanded the Maoists for killing

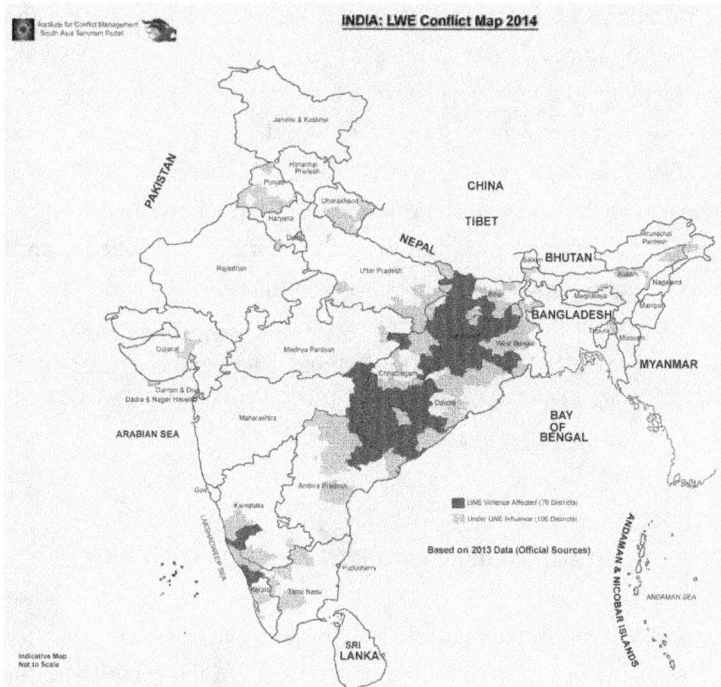

Figure 3.1 Conflict Zones

innocent citizens and declared herself against such violence. Yet in an interview to the magazine *Caravan* on 1 June 2010, she stated that those who have closely watched Maoists are clear that violence is the result of continuous injustice meted out to the common man, especially to the tribal people. Maoists have influence in the forests and tribal belts as in Lalgarh in West Midnapore district of West Bengal. This is a region, she said, which is inhabited by Dalits, Muslims and tribals, and in which the entire populace is below the poverty line. Nobody in Lalgarh possesses a ration card. States like Jharkand, Chattisgarh and Orissa, which provide bases for Maoism, are regions that sixty-five years after independence remain cut off from the development radar. People have been denied food, education, electricity, health facilities and basic amenities in these spaces. 'Yes, the middle class has appropriated these benefits, but not those who fall below the poverty line' she remarked.[5]

Into this political vacuum created by systemic social injustice, and shocking absence of remedial justice, have stepped the Maoists with their ideology of a new world geared towards the interests of the poor and the oppressed, their strategy of Peoples War, their long-term objective of taking over state power and their immediate objective of representing the needs of the disadvantaged through armed struggle. Though tribal communities throughout history have revolted against sundry people in positions of petty power, the Maoist struggle marks a new phase in the fight *of*, or more precisely the fight *for* the poor and the most disadvantaged. Isolated and often sporadic or random struggles have been welded together through the ideology and the strategy of revolutionary war.

Multiple disadvantages and revolution

The outbreak of armed struggle in these areas can best be explained as a response to a threefold failure: the failure of the central and the local state to deliver justice to territorially concentrated communities, the failure of the representatives of these communities to represent the plight of their constituents in various deliberative and decision-making forums and the failure of civil society organizations, campaigns and movements, particularly the dalit movement, to make the well-being of their own people who suffer from triple injustice their prime concern. The consequences of this triple failure to ensure redistribution, recognition and voice have been serious as we can see from the grim statistics on malnutrition, infant mortality, starvation and death.

That there is a link between multiple disadvantages and the outbreak of armed struggle was made clear by the 2009 draft report by Sub Group IV of the 'Committee on State Agrarian Relations and Unfinished Task of Land Reforms' set up by the Ministry of Rural Development, Government of India. The presence of the Naxalites in central India, continued the report, is a response both to past and to future land alienation, the failure of the government to live up to its constitutional mandate and the withdrawal of the state from its responsibility to protect the tribal realm.[6]

A year earlier, the 2008 report of the Expert Group set up by the Planning Commission, Government of India – 'Development Challenges in Extremist Affected Areas' – provided an even more stinging critique of policies and administration of tribal areas. Despite the plethora of development plans, programmes and activities, the majority of the STs live in conditions of serious deprivation and poverty, and they have remained backward in all aspects of human development including education, health and nutrition. Apart from social and economic deprivation, there has been a steady erosion of traditional tribal rights and their command over resources.[7] This is the belt most affected by Naxalite violence.[8]

At first glance, nothing seems to have changed since the Naxal movement broke out in 1967. A closer look, however, makes it clear that matters have worsened because of increasing commercial and industrial over exploitation of forestland and land alienation. Large tracts of land have been earmarked for industry or for Special Economic Zones. Above all, state governments have allowed the entry of mining companies into protected tribal lands. For the region termed the 'Red Corridor', which runs across Andhra Pradesh, Odisha, Chattisgarh, Bihar, Jharkand, Uttar Pradesh and West Bengal, possesses huge deposits of coal reserves, iron ore, bauxite and chromite. Entire communities have been stripped of their traditional rights, and escalating demands for these resources has displaced tribals in thousands. The Dandakaranya region, a forest area which borders four states Andhra Pradesh, Chattisgarh, Maharashtra and Orissa, and which covers three districts, Bastar, Kanker and Dantewada, has become one of the main sites for the seizure of land by state governments acting on behalf of the corporates.[9] The conclusion to chapter four (Alienation of Tribal and Dalit's Land) of the 2009 draft report by the government committee on State Agrarian Relations summed up the situation pithily, as the 'biggest grab of tribal lands after Columbus in the making'.[10] The script of the grab, continued the report, has been authored by corporates such as Tata Steel and Essar Steel, which wanted to mine the richest load of iron ore available in India.

In the first phase, the Naxalite movement had launched an armed struggle against usurious and exploitative landlords, corrupt officials and middlemen. In the current phase, the struggle is against dispossession and displacement, against appropriation of land that is the mainstay of livelihoods and against all sorts of agents from mining barons to middlemen intent on depriving tribals of their rights. The intrusion of mining companies into spaces held sacred by local communities such as the Niyamgiri hills, the destruction of the already fragile ecological balance of the region and forced and violent evictions from land have given rise to rampant discontent. It is this unrest that has been tapped by the Maoists.

Notably, earlier displacement of tribals and poor peasants was carried through in the name of some or the other public good, for instance the building of large irrigation projects to provide irrigation and power. Today, land is acquired by state governments and sold to corporates for private gain and profit. Nothing illustrates more the changing face of the Indian state and its participation in what has been called crony capitalism. In the process, the tribal community, which has a close and sustaining relationship with the forests, the land and water, has been dispossessed of the traditional resource base that enabled it to maintain bare life.

The Marxist geographer David Harvey has aptly termed this process 'accumulation by dispossession'. The Indian experience has overturned Marx's stage theories of capitalist growth. Primitive accumulation in which the producer is removed from her land and means of subsistence is no longer the pre-history of capitalism; it is an integral part of the process. Capitalism in its relentless search for profit searches for new sites for the exploitation of resources, even if these sites fall within protected zones.

And those who have been displaced will find no place in the organized working class, and they will find no place in a service economy that demands a different sort of skills. At the most, our displaced tribals and peasants might find uncertain daily jobs in the swelling construction industry, as exploited domestic labour, or as parking lot attendants. Far removed from their habitats, India's most neglected have been condemned to live in spaces that are far more desolate than their homelands. It is this sense of hopelessness and impending doom that the Maoists fight in today's India.

Conclusion

Each of the three stages of Naxalism possessed distinctive characteristics, romantic revolution in the first stage, dissipation of organization and energies in the second and a coming together of disparate organizations to fight massive land grabs for a capitalism that relentlessly preys on the lives of its people in the third. 'Accumulation, Accumulation' wrote Marx scathingly of acquisitive capitalists, 'this is their Moses and their Prophet'. How long do citizens of India have to lose their land, their livelihoods and their living spaces for the sake of a capitalism unbound? How long do we expect people to bear the combined weight of multiple injustices – economic deprivation, social discrimination and lack of voice – in democratic India? Even patience would climb down from her perch on the proverbial monument in rank frustration and sheer despair, even if she does not quite hasten to gather up the nearest AK47.

Considering the extent of ill-being that stalks the lives of the poor, considering that both the state and civil society groups have done little about ensuring well-being of the poorest of the poor, and considering that among the SCs and the STs living in central and east India there is more denial of self-respect, more infant mortality, more malnourishment, more ill health, more illiteracy and more premature deaths than the rest of the population, it is well-nigh impossible to definitively pronounce that violence is illegitimate. Premature deaths and ill-being could have been prevented, and it was within the power of the state to change their future. But nothing has been done and things worsened till the point the Maoists took up the cudgels. We have few defences against the revolutionary violence argument of the Maoists. Empirical facts prohibit the taking of uncompromising stands on political violence. But violence carries heavy costs, so we still ask – is revolutionary violence justified and if so why? It is to this that I now turn.

Can Revolutionary Violence Be Justified?

Introduction

The paradox of revolutionary violence is simply this. Scholars and analysts can understand and appreciate why people opt for revolutionary violence. Yet the costs that this form of politics carries in its wake are too heavy and cause unease. If we seek to justify revolutionary violence, we will have to make a stronger case than just triple disadvantage, or the ultimate objective of violence or even the prevention of greater harm. I argue in this chapter that the only circumstance in which revolutionary violence can be justified is overlapping injustice that betrays the basic presuppositions of a democratic state.

Contextual justification

Invoking images of brutality, of predators and of hapless victims, of savage violations of the body and damage to the mind, of crime, of dismemberment, of decapitation, of assault, of rape, of mutilation, of murder, of genocide, of ethnic cleansing and of other acts designed to maim and harm, violence, not surprisingly, is burdened by a great deal of moral overload. The question whether violence can ever be justified is one that is likely to evoke some astonishment, even a great degree of disparagement. It may well appear outrageous to some, and plainly irrelevant to others. Our interlocutors can protest with considerable outrage but perfect propriety that violence is a moral wrong; it can never ever be justified.

There is cause for unease with these absolutist moral stands. Do we really have to buy into the creed of political violence to acknowledge that in certain, and in very specific, circumstances violence can be justified? The justification of violence, to put the point across starkly, is context-dependent. One ready example that comes to mind is the infliction of some degree of harm to avert a larger harm. Picture someone who tries to forcibly prevent a child from rushing into a busy street and, in the process, inflicts injury upon the child. It will hardly be fair to the person, who has saved the child from serious harm, if we condemn her for exerting force when she pulled back the child and bruised the latter's forearm. A surgeon dexterously wields a knife to remove a malignant tumour and the patient suffers pain. This sort of harm can hardly be seen as a wrong because it is essential for the health of and the reasonable certainty of a longer life for the patient. Violence in such cases is certainly unavoidable.

Other circumstances come to mind. The police may be forced to fire on a gunman who holds a busload of children hostage. Axiomatically persons who perpetrate violence on others have to forfeit their own rights. If the state participates in, or sanctions or is inactive when a minority group is subjected to ethnic cleansing, surely the group under attack is justified in using violence to save the lives of members. Matters are different when it comes to, say, gang wars. There is nothing to justify violence here, not the context, not the objective and not lack of intention. In other cases cited above, violence is justified simply because there is no other way of preventing harm.

Violence, it follows, is not a mode of politics that lends itself to a general defence. It can be defended only with reference to the context, even as we acknowledge the high costs attached to violence. And that violence carries high costs is undeniable. The poet Amreeta Syam scripts an imaginary conversation between Subhadra married to the hero of the epic *Mahabharata* Arjun and Lord Krishna in the poem 'Kurukshetra'. The Great War of the *Mahabharata* has generally been understood as a war of the just against the unjust, a war of the righteous against the unrighteous. The human costs of the war were nevertheless beyond compare. It is precisely these costs that Subhadhra asks the God to account for. Because her young son Abhimanyu was brutally killed in the Great War, she in despair introduces a subversive note into the dialogue: 'This is a fight for a kingdom/-Of what use is a crown/ all your heirs are dead/When all the young men have gone/ ... And who will rule this kingdom/So dearly won with blood/A handful of old men/A cluster of torn hopes and thrown away dreams.'[1] The passage forces us to think: with what is society left after a civil war? Considering the sort of damage that is caused by violence, the issue of justification of this mode of politics has to be negotiated with some care and caution. We have to tread warily on great many eggshells to address the issue.

By reason of objectives

We could try to justify revolutionary violence in terms of its objectives. That is we could waive judgement on the costs of political violence because we endorse the purpose of the project: the creation of a social order based on equality and dignity for all. Faithful to the tradition of revolutionary war, we can argue that in a supremely unjust society violence has to be the midwife of history. There is simply no alternative. But this is a transitory phase. What will follow certain destruction is the equally certain birth of a new society tilted towards those who are poor and exploited and far removed from exploiters and potential exploiters. We can easily buy into the teleology of revolutionary guerrillas and support long-term interests against immediate costs such as harm.

The problem is that we just do not know. We have no way of knowing whether route V (violence) will lead to a preferred goal U (Utopia). Political predictions are hazardous at the best of time, and history teaches us that too many factors will, undoubtedly, intervene between the outbreak of political violence and the realization of the objectives of this form of violence. History after all brims over with best laid plans wrecked by contingency. Fortune, wrote Machiavalli, is the arbiter of one half of our actions. We can take precautions to protect ourselves against misfortune. But fortune 'shows her force where there is no organized strength to resist her; and she directs her impact there where she knows that dikes and embankments are not constructed to hold her'.[2] We also know of stories of political violence that lead nowhere except to the reproduction of violence. To justify violence in terms of its consequences might pave the way to political hell at worst and political imprudence at best. So, we will have to look elsewhere and appeal to other sorts of arguments to see whether they provide better sorts of justification of revolutionary violence. Can theories of political obligation and civil disobedience help us to justify revolutionary violence?

By reason of civil disobedience

In 399 BC, an Athenian jury found Socrates guilty of impiety and of corrupting the morals of the youth and ruled that he should be put to death by drinking hemlock. Thus was the death of a man widely regarded as the veritable fountainhead of philosophical reflection and wisdom scripted. On the eve of the execution, Crito and other friends visited Socrates and urged him to escape and take refuge somewhere else in order to avoid execution. The Socratic response to this plea in Plato's work *Crito* lucidly outlines why we ought to obey the laws of the state, or why we are bound by ties of political obligation.

What should I say, demands Socrates, if the community of the city-state of Athens comes before me and asks in some perplexity why I propose to run away on the eve of my execution? They have the right to ask this question, suggested the philosopher. For after all my stay in the city-state was proof enough that I was satisfied with my surroundings. They will remind me, Socrates tells Crito, that more than any other Athenian I stayed at home and hardly ventured out, apart from the one time I went to the Isthmus, to see the sights, or when I served in the army. They will hark back, he said, to the days when I showed absolutely no interest in knowing another city or other laws. 'We and our city' were sufficient for you. 'So vehemently were you choosing us and agreeing to be governed in accordance with us that among other things you also had children in it, as though the city was satisfactory to you'. Above all, they will tell me, Socrates admonishes his friend, that at the trial I could have chosen exile but I chose death. 'And you are doing' they will allege, 'what the paltriest slave would do: attempting to run away contrary to the contracts and agreements according to which you contracted with us to be governed. So first, answer us this very thing: whether what we say is true or not true when we claim that you have agreed in deed, but not in speech, to be governed in accordance with us'.[3]

A complex argument on why we obey the laws of the state is embedded in the heart of the Socratic response. Continued residence in a country and obedience to laws indicates that we tacitly accept the state as legitimate and as worthy of being obeyed. If we are unhappy, we can always opt for another country, another society and another set of laws. In the subsequent part of the response, Socrates noted that the state had begotten, nurtured and educated him just like a parent. For this, its citizens owed it gratitude and fidelity in the same way as one owes fidelity to parents.

The Socratic notion of political obligation anticipated contemporary explanations of why we obey the state by several centuries. Political theorists tell us that we are bound to obey the laws of the state simply because we accept benefits offered by the institution. We participate in a number of transactions within the framework set by the state. Above all, the freedom to choose one's representatives indicates tacit consent to obey the laws.[4] It follows that for Socrates, and for scholars who track his theoretical footprints, the question of disobeying the state does not arise, not really.

It is true that for the most part we obey the laws of the state we are born into, or the state we choose to live in, without greatly thinking or agonizing about it. But, there comes a time when many of us wonder why we should obey the laws of a state that has been found wanting. Why should we pay taxes when we know that massive thefts of public money line, nay pad the pockets of the representatives we elected to stand-in for us, and our interests, in legislative assemblies? Why should we obey laws of a government that watches in silence while thousands of its citizens are massacred and rendered homeless in communal and caste riots? Why should we obey a state that subjects its own citizens to triple disadvantage? And, why should we obey a state that enacts laws not worthy of being obeyed?

The dilemma to obey or not to obey a palpably immoral and unjust law was powerfully posed by Sophocles (495–406 BC) in his formidable play *Antigone*. Antigone daughter of Oedipus, who we have met earlier in this essay, defies the edict of King Creon of Thebes that her brother's corpse should not be entombed, and that it should be left for the birds and vultures to feast on. This act of disobedience has a history, as most acts of disobedience do. After the death of Oedipus, his two sons Eteocles and Polynieces battled for the throne, and both died during the course of the war. Their uncle Creon, brother of their mother Jocasta, ascended the throne of Thebes. He ordered that the defender of the city state, Eteocles, should be buried with honour. But no funeral rites should be performed for the aggressor Polynieces. Disregarding this palpably unfair law, Antigone performs the rituals of death and buries her brother's body with reverence and honour. Not surprisingly, Antigone is hauled up before a furious Creon: 'thou didst indeed dare to transgress that law'. Unfazed Antigone replies thus: 'Yes; for it was not Zeus that had published me that edict: not such are the laws set among me by the Justice who dwells with the gods below; nor deemed I that the decrees were of such force, that a mortal could override the unwritten and unfailing statutes of heaven. For their life is not of to-day or yesterday, but from all time, and no man knows when they were first put forth.'[5] Her justification for disobeying the laws of the state is simply this: when laws offend the rules and norms laid down by justice who dwells with the Gods, they are not worthy of being obeyed. Morality and the laws of God override man-made laws in every instance.

In Sophocles' power-packed play, Antigone anticipated an argument that a great man Gandhi was to make in the context of colonialism in the twentieth century. If laws violate the precept of natural justice, and if our conscience tells us that they are amoral or immoral, we have the natural right to follow the dictates of morality and disobey these laws.

Gandhi's philosophy, it well known, was heavily influenced by David Thoreau's reputed work on *Civil Disobedience*, which he seems to have read in 1907; that is a year after he had launched a protest against South African pass laws. Interestingly, civil disobedience does not imply that citizens should renege on political obligation or refuse to obey the state. On the contrary, for Gandhi, we must respect the legal system in the country. Nevertheless, we have the right to protest against a specific law that we are convinced is unjust in some way, or because it violates our considered moral convictions. What we do not do is to challenge the system of law. Therefore, we must readily accept punishment with good grace.

For Gandhi, moral judgement is infinitely higher than any law made by human beings. So we are perfectly right in disobeying a law that contravenes natural justice. The philosophy of satyagraha in Gandhian thought provides the foundation for civil disobedience against specific laws enacted by the state and against undesirable practices within the community. The satyagrahi's are moral exemplars. They have to prepare themselves for the task with dedication and humility. More significantly, the aim of satyagraha is not to humiliate or defeat the opponent but to convert him or her.

Can civil disobedience help us justify revolutionary violence? Perhaps not, because the theory presumes that the state is legitimate.

The argument can hardly help us justify revolutionary violence, which rejects the state. We will have to turn to other quarters to understand the political significance of rejecting the state.

By reason of self-defence

Most political theorists concur that the only time violence can be justified is in cases of self-defence or defence of others. We possess the fundamental and inalienable right not to be harmed, injured or killed. The corresponding proposition is as follows: if we injure or kill the person who intends to do us harm, we cannot be held culpable. Our right to life is of such overwhelming significance that it overrides the right to life of those who threaten us. Their right to life and to bodily integrity has simply lapsed. But while defending ourselves, we should take care that we do not use violence in excess of the violence used against us. Just that much, no more, measure for measure, not a penny less, nor a penny more. These arguments, which come mainly from the literature on just war, focus on the proportionality of violence used in primarily self-defence.

The right to defend oneself against attack has been reiterated by the Indian Supreme Court. In a recent case, the Court reminded Indian citizens that Parliament in enacting sections 96 to 106 of the Indian Penal Code 'clearly intended to arouse and encourage the manly [sic] spirit of self-defence amongst the citizens when faced with grave danger. The law does not require a law abiding citizen to behave like a coward when confronted with an imminent unlawful aggression ... there is nothing more degrading to the human spirit than to run away in face of danger'. The right of private defence, ruled the court, is designed to serve a social purpose and deserves to be fostered within prescribed limits.

The court went further than upholding the right to self-defence. Whereas the right to protect one's own person and property against unlawful aggression is an inherent right, we also have a duty to protect the person and property of others against such aggression. This duty, the court stated, is owed by man to society of which he is a member, and the preservation of which is both his interest and his duty.[6] In pursuance of this logic, the Supreme Court ruled that the accused had to satisfy the court that he was faced with an assault that caused a reasonable apprehension of death or grievous hurt, in order to be declared not guilty. The basic presumption of the ruling is that individuals can use violence to defend themselves and others against murderous attacks, only and only if no functionary of the state is around to protect them at that point of time and space. The right to self-defence is an individual right that can be used only in limited circumstances.

It follows that individual right to self-defence can be extended to a collective right of self-defence in, for example, cases of ethnic cleansing only and only if state structures have collapsed. Whether self-defence is a collective right in cases of genocide or ethnic cleansing, when the state has *not* collapsed but is merely inactive, is debatable. Whether this right can be used to register protest or in pursuance of a project to transform the state is even more debatable. The right to self-defence is not a right that a collective, an ethnic group or a revolutionary party can exercise against a state.

By reason of mandates

Arguably, revolutionary violence can be justified only and only if the state, which shapes the political context in which we live and work, has betrayed its mandate or violated the principles that grant it legitimacy in the first place. States are authorized to rule for specific purposes, notably the well-being of the people and protection of their interests. When states fail to discharge the mandate that has given them authority, arguably people have reason to revolt against the state.

This reasoning goes back to antiquity. In *Santi parva*, the twelfth episode of the epic *Mahabharata*, after the Great War the patriarch

Bhishma tutors the new monarch of Hastinapur, Yudhishtar, on the responsibilities of the ruler. Yudhishtar, convulsed with grief at the massive loss of lives, including that of his brother Karna, his sons and his nephews during the war, agonizes whether it is worthwhile to take up the reins of kingship. What he wonders is the point of power, if the path to this goal is drenched with the blood of his own people? 'Indeed' he ruminates, 'the whole Earth hath been subjugated by me ... This heavy grief, however, is always sitting in my heart, viz., that through covetousness I have caused this dreadful carnage of kinsmen'.[7]

He is advised to seek the advice of the patriarch Bhishma, master of the art of kingship who since the Great War has lain on a bed of vertically planted arrows, waiting for an appropriate time to order his own death. Yudhishtar approaching the great hero utters these words with some trepidation; 'persons conversant with duty and morality say that kingly duties constitute the highest science of duties ... Do thou, therefore, O king, discourse on those duties'.[8] Bhishma's discourse on kingly duties, or on *Raj-Dharma*, is known as the *Santi Parva*, a text that belongs to the genre of tutelage literature. Bhishma wends a leisurely way through advice on statecraft, and knowledge of geography, metaphysics, the cosmos, mythology, genealogy, history and Sankya and Yoga philosophy, to finally arrive at the question of what the ruler owes his people.

In section LIX of the *Santi Parva*, Yudhishtar asks Bhishma about the origins of kingship and of the symbol of power the *danda* or the sceptre. The reply to this question is familiar to all students of political theory, the deterioration of the original habitat of human beings that is the state of nature, and the social contract that rescues them from an increasingly insecure state, though the terminology is different. The commencement of sovereignty, according to Bhishma, begins with the degeneration of human beings, and their inability and their unwillingness to abide by the laws of *dharma*. 'At first there was no sovereignty, no king, no chastisement, and no chastiser. All men used to protect each other righteously.' But after some time, they began to find this task painful because perceptions of men came to be clouded by lust, by avarice and by covetousness. Virtue began to decline. 'And because men sought to obtain objects, which they did not possess, another passion called lust (of acquisition) got hold of them. When they became subject to lust, another passion, named anger, soon soiled them. Once subject to wrath, they lost all consideration of what should be done and what should not.' Righteousness was lost.[9]

The pre-political state of nature was not asocial, what it lacked was a ruler who could mediate and rule in conflict situations according to righteous laws. In another space, and at a time much later in history, John Locke was to similarly speak of the need for a state that could interpret and implement the law of nature. The *Santi Parva* not only anticipated John Locke but also Thomas Hobbes. Beset by greed, men in the pre-political state began to devour each other, a classic case of the big fish devouring small fishes – *matsyanyaya*. Overcome by fear, and wracked by uncertainty, a few inhabitants of the state of nature assembled and via divine intervention made certain compacts to regulate relationships with each other. Very soon, they realized that without a king who wielded the symbol of sovereignty and chastisement, the sceptre, they would be destroyed. Covenants without swords, as Hobbes was to write later, are mere words.

The Gods, says Bhishma to Yudhishtar, then created the institution of kingship for one main objective, the protection of the people. 'If there were no king on earth for wielding the rod of chastisement, the strong would then have preyed on the weak after the manner of fishes in the water.'[10] In return, the inhabitants of our pre-political state promise to give the ruler a fiftieth part of their animals and precious metals, and a tenth part of their grain, committed to offer him beautiful maidens who reach the age of marriage and also render to him a procession of accomplished men skilled in the use of weapons.[11] This commitment holds *as long* as the ruler, Bhishma tells Yudhishtar, rules in accordance with dharma.

At first glance, the concept of dharma is not very helpful, since dharma – understood basically as righteous conduct – applies as much to the individual as it does to society, and as much to inter-social relations as to the foundations of law and governance. In the *Mahabharata*, suggests philosopher Chaturvedi Badrinath, who has translated and interpreted the epic, concepts are not defined, because definitions are by their nature arbitrary. A concept is elaborated, understood and manifested in terms of its attributes or Lakshanas.[12] If we extrapolate from the generic concept of dharma, the attributes of kingly dharma are as follows.

The first property of *Raj-dharma*, *prabhavaya*, is that of nurturing, cherishing, providing more amply, endowing more richly, prospering, increasing and enhancing, in short providing for well-being and flourishing of the subjects. The second property of *Raj-dharma* is *dharna*, or holding-together, supporting, sustaining and bringing together all human beings. This particular aspect of *Raj-dharma* emanates from the philosophy of non-dualism or *Advaita*. According to this branch of Indian philosophy, human beings are neither separate from the divine, nor from each other. The other is a part of me as much as I am a part of her. It follows that if I hurt someone, I hurt myself; I violate my own integrity. In contrast to individualism, the Indian political philosophy tradition endorses a social and relational concept of the self. Not only is the construction of divisions between human beings or the forging of notions of 'us' and 'them' highly arbitrary, it is completely unnecessary. In order to complete ourselves as human beings, we have to recognize our connectedness with each other. This *Raj-dharma* must ensure. In political terms, the concept of dharana implies that a righteous king cannot sunder non-dualism by making artificial divisions between those who belong and those who do not.

The third property of *Raj-dharma* is that of non-violence or ahimsa.[13] The monarch has to protect the people from violence. In Indian philosophy, the notion of violence is closely connected to ignorance about our own nature and of our relationship to others and to the world. Enlightenment dissipates violence and enables us to choose between our propensity to violence and non-violence. Non-violence, therefore, cannot be seen as cowardice. Human beings make ethical choices when they chose non-violence over violence. In the aftermath of the Great War that caused suffering on an unprecedented scale, the *Santi Parva* places great importance on non-violence as the highest dharma and as the highest truth.

These three injunctions of *Raj-dharma* are part of a larger mission of the ruler. The king has to protect all creatures, even if he finds them odious. That is his rule has to be impartial. He is not expected to make any distinction whatsoever between his subjects. He protects them from external impediments such as threats of violence, but he also provides the preconditions of material flourishing. 'As the mother, disregarding those objects that are most cherished by her, seeks the good of her child alone, even so, without doubt, should kings conduct themselves (towards their subjects). The king that is righteous ... should always behave in such a manner as to avoid what is dear to him, for the sake of doing that which would benefit his people.'[14]

More significantly, if the purpose of the state is to protect the small fish from the big fish, the ruler must certainly not turn into the big fish himself. On the contrary, power is meant to protect the weak. The king who follows the path of dharma is the creator; the king who is sinful is the destroyer. The ruler should beware of exploiting the weak, for their eyes can scorch the earth. 'In a race scorched by the eyes of the weak, no children take birth. Such eyes burn the race to its very roots ... Weakness is more powerful than even the greatest Power, for that Power which is scorched by Weakness becomes totally exterminated.' 'If a person, who has been humiliated or struck, fails, while shrieking for assistance, to obtain a protector, divine chastisement overtakes the king and brings about his destruction.' The divine rod of chastisement falls upon the king. In injustice, a great destruction comes upon the king.[15]

The chief concern of dharmic political thought is the source of power, the objective for which power is exercised and the limits to power. It follows that if these limits are breached, revolt is justified. When dharma becomes adharma or that which is not dharma, or when oppression and violence follow abuse of power, then people who have entered into a contract with the ruler via divine intervention have the right to emancipate themselves from a rule that has not lived up to its own mandate. The rules of dharma are also rules on the limits of power. The rules of dharma are also the rights of the ruled to expect that the state will protect them without fear or favour.

The notion of protection in return for obedience looms large in theories of the social contract authored in seventeenth century England as well. Thomas Hobbes (1588–1679) and John Locke (1632–1704) argued that free men establish the state for certain purposes and objectives. Aristotle had told us that the state is the natural habitat of man. The social contract theorists performed a spectacular U-turn in political theory and suggested that the natural habitat of man is the state of nature. The state is an artificial creation, established to perform certain duties. Conversely, men are obliged to obey the state up to the point it abides by its mandate. Once the state lapses on its responsibilities, political obligation dissolves.

Locke grants to full members of the political community the power to remove the government if it does not abide by the terms of the original contract. Governments are dissolved when the legislature, or the prince, act contrary to the trust that the people have vested in them. Revolutions do not happen because of little mismanagement in public affairs. What people will not tolerate is abuse of power.

Great Mistakes in the ruling part, many wrong and inconvenient Laws and all the *slips* of human frailty will be *born by the People*, without mutiny or murmur. But, if a long train of Abuses, Prevarications and Artifices, all tending the same way, make the design visible to the People, and they cannot but feel, what they lie under, and see, whither they are going; 'tis not to be wonder'd, that they should then rouze themselves, and endeavour to put the rule into such hands, which may secure to them the ends for which Government was at first erected.[16]

Thomas Hobbes is considered to be a theorist of the absolutist state rather than a theorist of democracy. And yet even he grants to his individual the right to disobey the state if it violates its mandate. According to Hobbes, self-preservation, the basic instinct of human beings, is the chief reason for the establishment of the state in the first place. Accordingly, men retain the right to resist certain acts that will indisputably harm them. If the sovereign commands a man to kill, wound or maim himself, resist assaults or refrain from the use of food, air, medicine or any other item without which he cannot live, he has the liberty to disobey these commands. A subject has also the right *not* to go to war even if the sovereign commands him to do so, provided he can send someone else in his place, and provided the commonwealth is not under grave threat.

We see that there is more to self-preservation in the Hobbesian vision than the negative right not to be harmed. The sovereign cannot withhold any good that might harm the individual. The two sets of obligations, which serve to limit the power of the Hobbesian sovereign, correspond to what later came to called negative and positive obligations of the state. There are certain things a sovereign must *not do* to his subjects, for example torture or imprison them. And there are certain things that he *must do* for them: ensure that they do not die of thirst or malnutrition, lack of fresh air or uncured disease. Both these obligations are built into the contract that sets up the institution of sovereignty and endows it with legitimacy, and the ability to command obedience.

Hobbes goes further than this and writes the end of sovereign power is the safety of the people. By safety is not meant bare preservation but also access to all the 'contentments' of life, which every man by lawful industry, without danger, or hurt to the commonwealth, shall acquire to himself. That is the sovereign is obliged to protect the gains that men obtain through their own industry, on condition that that these gains have been acquired lawfully, and as long as economic activity does not harm the commonwealth. The Leviathan, in other words, must respect the property of his subjects.

What of men who are unable to acquire the 'contentments' of life for some reason or the other? Here Hobbes adds another twist to the tale of sovereign power. The monarch is obliged to protect people who cannot maintain themselves or their families and ensure that the poor do not have to depend on the charity of private persons. Hobbes, in sum, grants to his individual not only the right to resist any threat to bodily integrity, and the right to expect that the state will provide for him, but also that the state will respect the outcome of lawful labour. When certain classes of people cannot participate in economic transactions for some reason or the other, it is the duty of the state to take care of them. Expectedly, the obligation of the subjects to obey the sovereign lasts only as long as the power that protects them, and that ensures security, lasts. If it ceases, individuals have the right to take any action that is necessary for their self-preservation. This is one right, recollect, that has not been transferred to the state.[17] Though the jury is still out on the question of whether Hobbes grants to subjects the right to revolution, clearly he lays down limits on the rule of the Leviathan.

Democracy, justice and resistance

We get a glimpse of the mandate of the ruler, the principles upon which the state has been established, his obligations towards the people, the limits on power and the limits of political obligation. These obligations and limits are particularly strong in democracies for the simple reason that the body of citizens authorize the state to rule through express consent, notably vide the route of elections, and because fundamental rights, which are independent of a particular dispensation prescribe limits on state power.

The most significant fundamental right in a democracy is that of equality. The principle that forms the very presupposition of democracy – universal adult franchise – codifies the norm of equality, indeed it stands as a metaphor for equality. Equality as a palpably moral norm codifies a powerful presumption: the equal moral worth of persons. Persons are equal because each human being has certain capacities in common with other human beings, for instance the capacity to make their own histories in concert with other similarly endowed human beings. Of course, the histories that persons make might not be the histories they chose to make, but this is not the issue at hand. What is important is that each person possesses this ability.

The principle of equal moral worth generates at least two robust principles of political morality. First, equality is, morally speaking, a default principle. Any deviations from the norm have to be justified by the state. Therefore, and this is the second postulate, persons should not be discriminated against on grounds such as race, caste, gender, ethnicity, disability or class. These features of the human condition are morally irrelevant.

If someone were to ask 'equality *for* what', we can answer that equality assures equal moral worth and hence equal standing of persons, and that equal standing is an essential precondition for participation in the multiple transactions of society. For example when we line up to exercise our franchise in the neighbourhood polling station, our vote is as equal as that of the 'man' next door, even if he is far wealthier and far more privileged than we are. The precept of political equality logically implies that we should be able to participate in economic, cultural, social and political transactions on the same basis as we cast our vote. In, for instance, public deliberations, my voice has to be given as much weight as my neighbour who is so much more wealthy and powerful than I am. If he is given more importance simply because he is richer, my standing is diminished.

The significant point is that different forms of equality, political, economic and social are not distant cousins; they are constitutive of democracy itself. Yet, most democracies easily live with basic contradictions in society; political equality and social and economic inequality. We hardly require a colourful or an overripe imagination to comprehend that social and economic disparities spill over into the political domain and hamper political equality. The poor are not only likely to be socially marginalized, humiliated, dismissed and subjected to intense disrespect in and through the practices of everyday life, but also rendered politically insignificant in terms of the politics of 'voice' as distinct from the 'vote'. And now consider the power of wealth; politicians use money to buy votes, the owners of capital buy politicians and the media owned by powerful houses of capital shapes public opinion in 'this' or 'that' image.

No conception of democracy can ignore the fact that social disparities greatly inhibit the realization of the basic principle of democracy – political equality. Therefore, if the democratic state wishes to ensure that political equality is not compromised by social and economic inequality, it has to provide basic social goods, such as education, health, shelter and remunerative employment to its citizens. Though all citizens have a right to these goods, the state has a special responsibility to those people who are unable to participate in the transactions of the market.

For many policy planners, the market is the answer to all our problems. They overlook that the institution of the market is supremely amoral inasmuch as it is completely indifferent to those cannot buy, and those who find no buyers for what they sell, for example their labour. It is precisely at this point that the democratic state is expected to step in and provide social goods to people on non-market principles. The failure of the state to do so results in the production of new inequalities and the reproduction of old ones.

A rider needs to be inserted here. The objective of redistributing resources is not only that people should get just so many resources, precisely so much cash, exactly so much education and specifically so much health care. Access to resources is important because these resources allow people to participate as equals in the various transactions of society from the household to the state. If they are subjected to extreme deprivation and discrimination, and if they do not have voice, their ability to do so peters out. This diminishes human beings. Equality is a relational concept, and if people cannot participate in transactions from a position of equality, we have the spectre of lessened, devalued and demoralized human beings on our hands.

By reasons of democratic justice

Redistribution of resources to provide basic needs to every person is also crucial for the realization of justice. Justice is not exclusive to democracy, for every tyrant seeks to legitimize unacceptable acts by reference to some or the other notion of justice. Logically, in democratic societies, justice codifies and reflects the basic precept of democracy and the reason why this form of government is seen as legitimate: equality. The principle of democratic justice, condensing as it does the norm of equality, holds that each person has an equal right to share in the benefits of society. By the same logic, no one can be compelled to bear more than her fair share of the burdens of that society. The benefits and the burdens of society, in short, have to be distributed as equally as possible.

If this principle is violated in any way, by deep-rooted inequalities for instance, citizens have the right (vide freedom of expression and the right to form associations) to prise open political norms for debate and re-negotiation in civil society. In most societies, secularism and religion in the public sphere, equality and egalitarianism, freedom and license, constitutional and moral rights, gender rights, the rights of sexual minorities and notions of remedial and retributive justice are the subject matter of intense debate and often-fraught confrontations. Some of these debates fall within accepted parameters of democracy and justice. Others do not, become a matter of controversy and have to be thrashed out in the domain of civil society and/or the judiciary. Such debates, howsoever unresolved or disjoined they may be, are politically momentous in so far as (a) they validate the equal right citizens have to participate in the making of decisions and (b) reiterate the right of citizens to debate on the norms of justice.

In other words, in democracies, citizens have the basic right to 'voice'. We can vote out a particular regime through careful and strategic use of the franchise. We can participate in collective action in civil society, build up informed public opinion and compel the government to heed us. We can tap the energies of civil liberty activists to help safeguard lives and liberties. We can approach the judiciary and appeal to constitutional provisions to defend cases of violations of civil liberties. We can agitate, take out processions, demonstrate, undertake fasts and use the media to protest against undemocratic and unjust laws. And we can pillory the state at the bar of international opinion. But this is possible only if we have voice or a presence in civil society.

If identifiable groups are unable to participate in these transactions simply because their members are trapped in double disadvantage and injustice, they have been treated unjustly. Double injustice acquires an added dimension of injustice when members of these groups are deprived of voice in the public domain of politics, and thereby denied the opportunity of bringing influence to bear upon the state through collective action. If they had voice, their plight might not have been quite as acute as it is today. But it is precisely this right of participation in public debate as equals, or the right to voice beyond elections, that is denied to the poor who are already deprived and discriminated against. The denial bears grim implications, for if people are denied voice, they are deprived of the opportunity to protest against violations of social and civil rights.

Let us now confront the question that lies at the heart of this argument. If in a democracy, for example India, sections of people are locked into triple injustice, are they still bound to obey the state? If extreme deprivation persists, if social discrimination is continuously reproduced and if groups lack voice as distinct from the vote, do people not have the right to pick up arms against a state that has lapsed on its own mandate and betrayed democracy? Perhaps they have no other option. These options are either not available or have been exhausted.

Note that it is not only extreme deprivation and/or social discrimination, which justifies revolutionary violence; the crucial factor that justifies this form of politics is *lack of voice*. If people cannot participate in public discussions and claim that they bear a disproportionate share of the burdens of a society, and that they have not been given access to a fair share in the benefits of a society, this constitutes serious betrayal of the basic concept of democratic justice.

Is this reason enough to justify revolt against the state? Prima facie, we are compelled to agree that in circumstances stamped by triple injustice revolutionary violence can be justified.

Conclusion

Revolutionary violence can be defended on three grounds. First, we can justify Maoist violence in terms of long-term goals. The problem is that we simply do not know whether these goals will ever be achieved. Second, we can see what the limits of political obligation and reasons for civil disobedience against the state are. But civil disobedience does not involve rejection of the state. And it is precisely this rejection that constitutes the central plank of the revolutionary agenda. The third ground for justification is self-defence. However, whether this right can be used against the state as a mark of protest, or in pursuance of a project to transform the state, is debatable.

The political context that allows us to see revolutionary violence as prima facie justified is the production and reproduction of triple disadvantage and injustice. This infringes the basic principles of democratic justice three times over. In India, the inability of the triply disadvantaged to participate in public debates on re-negotiating justice is a damming comment on the failure of the democratic states to institutionalize justice, that is, ensure a fair share of the benefits and burdens of society to each citizen. It is an equally damming comment on the ability of the democratic state to live with the fact that millions of people in poverty-stricken areas have been compelled to shoulder a disproportionate share of the burdens of society. They do not share in the benefits of this society, and they do not have voice in the public deliberations of civil society or in collective action. In addition, they have become targets of state violence that ranges from torture, to encounter deaths, to mass graves, to killings of innocent people.

Social injustice deprives citizens of their due right to participate in the multiple transactions of their society with a sense of self-worth, and state violence deprives them of their basic civil liberties, notably the right to life. Above all, people lack voice. This is a serious infringement of the basic precepts of democracy, because all roads to justice are, thereby, blocked. If they pick up the gun and aim it against the state and its officials, or if they support a group that struggles for a just society, is this prima facie justified? A prima facie 'yes' might be in order here. But this is not the end of the story. Even if we justify revolutionary violence with reference to the context of triple injustice, an exploration and evaluation of this form of politics remains on our agenda.

The Ambiguities of Political Violence

Introduction

Revolutionary violence, it has been suggested in the previous section, can be prima facie defended in a very specific set of circumstances, the overlap between three avatars of injustices – social discrimination, extreme deprivation and lack of voice. Let me as a prelude to the argument below reiterate briefly the distinguishing feature of revolutionary violence. This avatar of violence is distinguished by, at least, three features. First, the proponents of revolutionary violence believe that in deeply unequal societies such as India, the grip of threefold injustice upon the lives of people is intractable and can be broken only through acts that involve coercion. Second, revolutionaries renounce political obligation to the state, but they do not renege on moral obligation to the rest of the citizens. They seek to replace a state that has displayed remarkable and a somewhat stunning incapacity to provide justice to its citizens, with one that will be responsive to precisely those people who have been abandoned on the sidewalks or consigned to the ditches of the pathway treaded by history. Third, revolutionary violence in the form of guerrilla war is less about the use of instruments of force and destruction and more about the political mobilisation of, in particular, the constituency on whose behalf the group has picked up arms and, in general, society.

The last is a necessary precondition for guerrilla war. Strategically, armed guerrillas fighting an unconventional war have to rely on the support of constituencies to provide assured sanctuaries, information and sustenance. Politically, people within and without the constituency should be convinced of the need for and of the rightness of the cause. It is only then that they can, metaphorically, stand up and speak back to a history not of their making. The objective of revolutionary violence is to transform the politics of voicelessness into the politics of voice. For those of us who prefer politics in the progressive mode, revolutionary violence proves a far better bet for the recovery of agency through the repossession of voice than other forms of politics.

Grey areas in revolutionary politics

Even so a great deal of ambiguity proscribes clear and unconditional endorsement of this particular mode of politics. We simply cannot turn a blind eye to the multiple pitfalls that disfigure the preferred route to political Utopia in the imaginaries of the revolutionaries. Etched starkly onto the political horizon, in blazing alphabets of mayhem and gore, are the costs of violence unleashed by the state, as well as by our revolutionaries. So many lives lost, so many innocent people killed, so much arson, so much destruction of public property, so much turmoil and so much insecurity. The condition of people living in regions of India that the Maoists have made their base is nothing short of the Hobbesian state of nature – 'nasty, brutish and short'.

Apart from carrying out indiscriminate killing of persons targeted as police informers, moneylenders and forest officials, the Maoists have been deeply compromised, charged as they are with extortion, and accused as they are of terrorizing local populations, of demanding shelter and succour at gun point, of destroying school buildings, railways, health facilities and government establishments and of creating an atmosphere of rank dread. Children between the age of 6 and 12 years are, reportedly, recruited for combat operations, indoctrinated ideologically, used as informers, trained to fight with sticks and other weapons and employed to loot armouries and purchase explosives. Viewed from this vantage point, the appeal of an ideology and strategy of a revolutionary political agenda appears greatly reduced. The glitches in using violence in often irresponsible and disproportionate ways appear starkly visible and much less defensible.

Let us frontally confront the paradox of revolutionary violence. As responsible citizens of the Republic of India, we recognize the sheer stubbornness of particularly vicious forms of injustice. Prima facie, there seems to be no way out of this spiral of injustice, suffering and state-sponsored violence, except revolutionary violence. As persons capable of making informed political judgements, we might also accept that revolutionary violence is far preferable to other forms of 'violence as protest' simply because the avatar acknowledges moral responsibility not only to one creed, region or language, but to the impoverished and vulnerable people. Contrasted with other users of political violence bent on extracting concessions from the state for their group and their group alone, revolutionary violence aims to not only redress institutionalized injustice, but also to fundamentally transform state and society so that all people can live and work in a context free of everyday humiliation and vulnerability.

The paradox is that this mode of politics need not always add up to political wisdom or marked by prudence. It is bad politics to wave away losses of human lives, and destruction of habitations as collateral damage, and focus on the goal instead. It is also completely unethical. For we cannot, ever, be confident that the objective for which the guerrillas have picked up arms will ever be attained. None of us, not even a prescient and exceptionally gifted fortune-teller, can predict with certainty that the route of violence *will* lead to the desired goal and nowhere else. Despatches from history tell us that contingency and fortune is the name of the game.

Evaluating revolutionary violence

I am, note, not bringing into the argument the consideration that violence is a moral bad. Certainly, violence is a moral bad, but multiple injustices under which some of our own people quake are also a moral bad. The issue is different. Even if we justify revolutionary violence with reference to the immediate context as has been done in the previous section of the essay, this cannot be the end of the story. We cannot exempt revolutionary violence from political judgements on the basis of the here and now and ignore the wider dimensions of the issue. As a form of politics, revolutionary violence impacts our collective existence. Our collective lives are shaped by the political context we live and work in, in association with others, and our choices are enabled or circumscribed by this context. We cannot possibly be indifferent to acts of the state as well as of non-state actors that impress this context with their brand of politics.

Moreover, as members of a political community, we hold obligations to our fellow citizens. If they have come to harm, we need to engage with the state that has seriously lapsed on its responsibility to citizens. But, at the same time, we also need to engage with the revolutionaries who pick up the gun on behalf of the vulnerable and the deprived. There is need to politically evaluate the efficacy of revolutionary violence as a means of achieving given objectives.

In any case, are political theorists not bound to adjudicate this avatar of politics much in the way we evaluate other forms of politics from collective action, to political parties, to the high politics of the state? Why not? Political practices, especially those that carry great costs, cannot be their own defendant, judge and jury. They have to be judged on some criterion because they impact our collective lives deeply. Concerned observers and analysts have to be Janus-faced, with one face turned towards the state and its policies and the other towards political practices in society. But, then, we must be reasonably sure of how to evaluate practices in the violent mode or violence in the revolutionary mode.

On balance, we can and do evaluate politics and political practices from different vantage points, the ends a specific practice espouses, its tactics, its conventions and its procedures of mobilization. If as democrats we are committed to equality, we should be assessing political practices by reference to the following question. Does a particular mode of politics enable vulnerable people to 'stand up', speak back to a history that is not of their making and thereby acquire agency? It is vitally important that politics in the transformative mode should aspire to a society in which people, particularly the most disadvantaged, are actors or agents in their own right, and that they can participate in the multiple transactions of society from a position of confidence. In a society stamped by inequality, oppression and injustice, democratic politics is about facilitating and catalysing the transition from subject to agent.

The proviso is that leaders or aspirant leaders can be, in the political battlefield, only catalysers and facilitators. They cannot force people to believe 'this' rather than 'that'. Ultimately, it is the people who decide and realize agency because they make choices. A passionate desire to transform society and rid it of all warts and flaws may well throw up the option of revolutionary violence. This cannot be ruled out. What is important is that people must have political choices. They must know what they pick up arms for, why they should support the objective of this form of politics and what the problems of revolutionary violence are. They should be able to speak back to society, but they should also be able to speak back to the sort of politics that enables this sort of power.

Accordingly, when we as democrats set out to evaluate political practices whether of collective action or of revolution, we ask whether a particular sort of politics has allowed individuals and groups to exercise or to recover agency. Politics is not judged only by the goals it defends as its rationale and chief legitimacy claim because we may never reach there, but on the basis of what political practices do for ordinary people, and what they do not do for them.

Therefore, I suggest that instead of resorting to empty and sanctimonious arguments on the immorality of violence we should proceed to investigate revolutionary violence from its own parameters, its principles and its conventions, and not from a moral standpoint outside the practices of violence. This will enable us to judge whether the main presupposition of revolutionary violence; that of giving the marginalized agency, are borne out by strategies of revolutionary war.

Reclaiming selfhood I

In deeply hierarchical and unjust societies, does revolutionary politics as praxis enable people who are triply disadvantaged to recover agency and make their own histories. Of course, the history ordinary people make might not be the history they wanted to make in the first instance, or they might make these histories badly. But that is not the main issue, the issue is whether people have claimed voice. Have people, who for decades have laboured under the multiple burdens that our unjust history has placed on their shoulders, recovered agency through political practices? Do they need to resort to violence to do so or support those who wield AK47s?

Take the case of India. Sumanta Bannerjee, who styles himself a one-time Maoist, suggests that the objective of the earlier Naxalite movement was not only to assure access to basic material goods, but also to secure justice and equal treatment for the landless labourer and the tribal. The Naxalites, he suggests, gave back dignity to the downtrodden peasantry, which had been socially discriminated against and exploited for centuries. In a world where the upper-class landlords treated the 'doubly disadvantaged' as untouchables, denied them civic rights and had no compunction in abducting and raping their women, Naxalite politics inspired precisely these people to assert themselves as equal human beings. Revolutionary violence enabled them to resist humiliating codes of conduct imposed by the upper castes. He cites the voice of an old Bauri (depressed class) peasant in a village in Burdwan district who said in 1969 that Naxalbari had authorized him to walk with his head held high. He no longer had to make way for the upper castes when they crossed his path.[1]

In a similar vein, George Kunnath, who has carried out considerable fieldwork in Bihar, seems to suggest that violence, involving very often the killing of notorious landlords and moneylenders, occupation and redistribution of land, imposition of fines and summary executions, might well be necessary precondition of the recovery of self-respect.[2]

In the mid twentieth century Frantz Fanon, the author of the celebrated work 'The Wretched of the Earth' had made much the same argument.[3] Born in the Caribbean, in the French colony of Martinique in 1925, Fanon was greatly influenced by his celebrated teacher Aime Cesaire. Cesaire's volume of essays, *Discourse on Colonialism*, had quickly attained the status of a classic, and he became famous as the founder of the intellectual and ideological movement *Negritude* that celebrated blackness. At a very young age, Fanon was exposed to the savage racism of the French army stationed in the island. At the age of 18, he left Martinique and fought with the Free French Forces in the Second World War. After the end of the war, he stayed on in France to study medicine and psychiatry in Lyons. The intellectual atmosphere in France in that period was shaped by the existentialism of Jean Paul Sartre and the phenomenology of Merleau-Ponty, by Hegel and by Marx. These intellectual streams of thought deeply impacted Fanon.

In 1952, Fanon took up the position of chief of staff for the psychiatric ward of Bida-Jonville hospital in Algeria. In 1954, the series of attacks launched against military and civilian targets by the Front de Liberation Nationale (FLN) heralded the Algerian war of independence. Within a period of four years, Fanon deeply critical of French policy towards Algeria resigned from his job and dedicated himself to the cause of the FLN. Algeria was liberated from French rule in July 1962, seven months after Fanon's death from leukaemia. His *Wretched of the Earth* was published posthumously. Till today, it is seen as a classic that dwells not only on the production and reproduction of violence under colonialism, but also on the violence of the post-colonial elite and resultant loss of hope.

In this much acclaimed work, Fanon brings out in fine detail the subtleties and the power of violence, as well as its waywardness. He wrote elegantly and powerfully of the crippling effects of settler colonialism on the collective psyche of the colonized. The reach of violence, he theorized, is widespread, timeless and enduring. Footprints of the cloven hoof of violence are practically ineradicable. It is perhaps not surprising that the post-colonial elite cannot, but, be cast in the mould of the same violence it had led the struggle against. The colours of violence do not wash out quite so easily.

But violence, theorizes Fanon, is double edged, both lethal and liberating at the same time. The violence of settler colonialism hammers the colonized into submission. Logically, the only way 'natives' can speak back to a history that has enslaved their minds and bodies is to use the weapon of the colonizer against him. This may even be advantageous because violence enables the 'native' to shrug off the crippling inferiority complex produced by colonialism. Violence rescues natives from inertia, restores their self-respect and enables men to recover 'manhood' translated as agency. 'At the level of individuals, violence is a cleansing force. It frees the native from his inferiority complex and from his despair and inaction; it makes him fearless and restores his self-respect. Even if the armed struggle has been symbolic, and the nation is demobilised through a rapid movement of decolonisation, the people have the time to see that the liberation has been the business of each and all and that the leader has no special merit.'[4] The form of violence adopted by the colonized is reactive but nevertheless beneficial. Violence develops consciousness of a common cause, of a national destiny and of a collective history.[5]

The theme of violence as liberation was highlighted in the preface to the *Wretched of the Earth* written by Jean Paul Sartre. 'When the peasants lay hands on a gun, the old myths fade, and one by one the taboos are overturned; a fighter's weapon is his humanity. For in the first phase of the revolt killing is a necessity; killing a European is killing two birds with one stone, eliminating in one go, oppressor and the oppressed; leaving one man dead and the other man free, for the first time the survivor feels a national soil under his feet.'[6] Fanon too is clear about the advantages that violence delivers into the hands of the colonized, notably recovery of the self.

Reclaiming selfhood II

The passionate advocacy of violence as a tool of emancipation is, however, only one part of the story Fanon told the world. The paralysing influence of colonialism can be broken only through the use of violence. This is incontrovertible. Spontaneous violence has its uses, but it can be self-defeating; it can subvert liberation. You do not carry on a war, he wrote, nor suffer brutal repression, nor look on while all other members of your family are wiped out in order to make hatred triumph. But '[r]acialism and hatred and resentment – "legitimate desire for revenge" – cannot sustain a war of liberation. Those lightning flashes of consciousness which fling the body into stormy paths or which throw it into an almost pathological trance where the face of the other beckons me on to giddiness, where my blood calls for the blood of the other, where by sheer inertia my death calls for the death of the other-that intense emotion of the first few hours falls to pieces if it is left to feed on its own substance'.[7] Not only do hatred and bloodlust peter out within a short span of time, 'hatred alone cannot draw up a programme'.

At this point in the argument, Fanon warns against excessive or sole reliance on violence. This course of action, he suggests, is hardly prudent, politically speaking. Unless those who wield violence are clear about the purpose of what they are doing, they tend to capitulate easily to the blandishments of the settler. The objectives of the struggle ought not to be chosen without discrimination, Fanon tells us, for people might begin to question the prolongation of the war the moment the enemy offers concessions. So seductive is the need to be recognized as a human being that the 'native' can easily cave in.[8] The headiness of the gun is replaced by another sort of headiness; that of being recognized as a human being by the very people who had denied to the Algerians humanity. People engaged in liberating themselves from brutal colonialism must not imagine that the fight is won by these small concessions; their demands must not become modest. Placated easily by meaningless sops, the revolution will certainly collapse and the recovery of agency through violence will prove short-lived.

Hatred for Fanon is not a political agenda; it can never be an agenda, just one temporary and dispensable milestone on the route to liberation. The users of violence have to be constantly patrolled; the use of violence has to be moderated and educated by the leaders. The activist and the leader must take control. 'Once again, things must be explained to them; the people must see where they are going, and how they are going to get there.' Politics has to control violence otherwise the entire project of liberation can go haywire. In order to prevent this, in order to politicize people into the intricacies of the issue at hand, the war has to continue, but not as a project of violence but of that as politics.

The task of bringing the people to political maturity demands certain preconditions: the political organization leading the revolt must be structured thoroughly, and leaders must exhibit a high degree of intellectual excellence. The task of party vanguard is not easy, it has to educate people so that they can take stock of a situation, it has to enlighten consciousness, and also advance knowledge of history and society.[9] Revolutionary elements, which form the embryonic political organization of the rebellion, argues Fanon, have to establish a mutual current of enlightenment and enrichment with the people. It is only then that in each fighting group, and in every village, people who have begun to 'splinter upon the reefs of misunderstanding [can] be shown their bearings by these political pilots.... Such a taking stock of the situation at this precise moment of the struggle is decisive, for it allows the people to pass from total, undiscriminating nationalism to social and economic awareness.'[10]

Hatred alone cannot draw up a programme, wrote Fanon, cautioning us against excessive reliance on violence as the architect of history. Spontaneous and passionate outbursts of violence will disintegrate if the users of violence do not graduate to a different level of political consciousness. A transformative agenda can be created only when people seek horizons hitherto undreamt of, horizons that are beyond violence. If nationalism 'is not enriched and deepened by a very rapid transformation into a consciousness of social and political needs ... it leads up a blind alley', writes Fanon in the chapter on 'the Pitfalls of National Consciousness'.[11] In the concluding paragraph of the chapter on 'Spontaneity: Its Strengths and Weaknesses' Fanon pens this politically significant sentence '[v]iolence alone, violence committed by the people, *violence organised and educated by its leaders*, makes it possible for the masses to understand social truths and gives the key to them'.[12]

Though Fanon has been conceptualized as *the* theorist of an unreflective and muscular violence, which is a means of recovering agency, his theory, we see, is much more nuanced. Colonial violence stripped the colonized of self-respect. They wilted before the sheer brutality of colonialism. In the specific context of dehumanization and disempowerment, Fanon sees violence as the only way out of the impasse. The arrogance of the settler cannot be broken by any other means; the agency of the colonized cannot be recaptured in any other way. But violence, warns Fanon, has to be viewed instrumentally, as a mode of recovering agency, as a mode of connecting to others and as a mode of constituting a collective. Violence confers power on its users, but power in the abstract can turn out to be a mirage, an illusion. For these reasons and more, violence for Fanon is not a political programme; its use has to be constantly patrolled, controlled and educated by the leaders. Politics have to control violence otherwise the entire project of liberation will collapse. The proper aim of liberation is to destroy the circle of violence and counter-violence, to destroy the exploitation of existing elites as well as the potential project of exploitation by future elites, and to fashion another sort of politics. The psychic and physical costs of perpetrating uncontrolled violence are far too high.

Fanon, always the psychiatrist, understands and appreciates that for the colonized and the subjugated violence might appear to be the only mode of regaining selfhood. When there is no archive outside the one fashioned by the violence of the ruling elites, whether colonial or postcolonial, it is easy for people to opt for violence as a resolution to what they perceive as a problem. But rather than being a solution to problems, unrestrained violence is a problem in itself. In suggesting that violence needs to be channelled and restrained by another form of politics, Fanon tells us that though violence cleanses, there is also a politics outside violence. The politics of violence cannot be allowed to transform itself into a permanent mode of violent politics. Much as the argument in this essay theorizes political violence contextually, for Fanon the advocacy of violence is purely contextual.

We have to learn from Fanon when we set out to evaluate revolutionary violence in cases such as India. It is true that picking up the gun to confront the agents of the state and upper castes for whom suppression and exploitation of the so-called lower castes and tribals is an unquestioned creed, and for whom the marginalization of these groups is neither here nor there, appears justified. When the upper castes show no compassion, no solidarity, no pity, no charity, let alone consciousness of human rights, and when they lack vision of what it means to be human, what does one expect the oppressed to do, except try to reshape society? Yet, the benefits of violence are limited.

Preconditions of guerrilla war

At an earlier time and another place, Mao Zedong, the architect of China's revolution against semi-feudalism and semi-colonialism, said much the same thing about revolutionary violence. Mao Zedong's contribution to the theory of revolutionary violence, which we can safely assume is both the Talmud and the Bible for Maoist revolutionaries, is well known. He overturned the Marxist theory of revolution and proceeded to stand it on its head, much like Marx had stood Hegel's theory of history on its head. Taking China as his empirical referral, he argued that predominantly agrarian countries lack a working class which, or so it is expected by Marxist orthodoxy, is endowed with political consciousness of exploitation and alienation. In agrarian societies, it is the peasantry that is politically significant. In semi-feudal countries, where the hold of landlords over landless peasants and small cultivators is particularly stark and brutal, revolution can only come through guerrilla or unconventional war, either waged by the peasants or supported by this class.

Notably, guerrilla war is not specific to Maoism. In the immortal classic *War and Peace*, Leo Tolstoy evocatively and powerfully describes how segments of the Russian army and civilian groups harassed Napoleon's army. The latter was in full retreat from a Moscow that had been burned to the ground.

> One of the most conspicuous and advantageous departures from the so-called rules of warfare is the independent action of men acting separately against men huddled together in a mass... In this kind of warfare, instead of forming in a crowd to attack a crowd, men disperse in small groups, attack singly and at once fly, when attacked by superior forces, and then attack again when an opportunity presents itself... Such were the methods of the guerrillas in Spain; of the mountain tribes in the Caucasus, and of the Russians in 1812.

Thousands of retreating soldiers of the French army under the command of Napoleon were slain by Cossacks and the peasants. The latter killed French soldiers as instinctively as dogs set upon a stray mad dog, wrote Tolstoy. The irregulars destroyed the *Grandee Armee* piecemeal. By October, when the French were fleeing to Smolensk, hundreds of these companies, some detachments following the usual routine of the army, some consisting of only Cossacks, others of mounted men and bands of men on foot, and still others consisting of peasants or of landowners and their serfs stalked the retreating army. Concluding his account of the retreat of the French army from Russia, Tolstoy tells us that the country was cleared of the invaders primarily because the flight was promoted by irregular warfare. Guerrillas wrecked the French army. It was also obliterated by the Great Russian army following in the rear of the French, ready to use force in case there was any pause in their retreat.[13]

Guerrilla techniques of warfare have been employed against invaders, against colonial powers, against autocratic regimes and sometimes against democratic regimes as well. In the middle of the twentieth century in South America, a specific variant of guerrilla war, the Foco Theory, is associated with the name of Che Guevara. Born in village Rosario in Argentina in 1928 as Ernesto Guevara de la Serna, Che Guevara or simply the iconic Che, whose face today adorns T-shirts worn with designer jeans, gained immense fame as a theorist, as a tactician of guerrilla war, as an anti-imperialist and as a left radical who played a significant role in the Cuban revolution from 1956 to 1959. Travelling across the continent of South America as a young man, Che came to the conclusion that the only way out of the morass of poverty that saturated and diminished the lives of millions of people in South America was a continent-wide violent revolution.

In the 1950s, he met the two brothers Fidel and Raul Castro in Mexico. The brothers were planning to overthrow the dictatorship of Fulgencio Batista in Cuba. Che joined the force put together by Fidel Castro, and in the region of Sierra Maestra in Cuba, he constructed a nucleus of a guerrilla army to fight the dictatorship. It took two years for the guerrillas to overthrow the Batista government. In 1966, he went to Bolivia incommunicado to create and lead a guerrilla group in the region of Santa Cruz. In October 1967, the group was annihilated by a special detachment of the Bolivian army. Che was captured and shot.

In 1960, Che had published an extremely influential manual *La Guera de Guerrillas* or *Guerrilla Warfare*. This work on armed struggle was augmented by another work, *Guerrilla Warfare: A Method and a Message to the Tricontinental*. Che argued that unconventional war, which aims to capture political power, is a people's war and any attempt to carry out this war without the support of the population will be a prelude to inevitable disaster. The guerrilla band is an armed nucleus; 'it draws its great force from the mass of the people themselves'.[14] The guerrilla, he went on to argue, is a social reformer, the war gives voice to the angry protests made by people against their oppressors, and he fights to change the social system that keeps his unarmed brothers in ignominy and misery. 'He launches himself against the conditions of the reigning institutions at a particular moment and dedicates himself with all the vigor that circumstances permit to breaking the mold of these institutions.'[15]

The Cuban revolution, he suggested, made three fundamental contributions to the laws of revolutionary movement. First, people's forces can win a war against the army, second, it is not necessary to wait until all conditions for making revolution exist, and third, armed fighting in underdeveloped countries has to be in the countryside.[16] Che's interpretation of Marxist theories of revolution to fit the specific conditions of South America proved highly influential. His eclectic theory of revolutionary war was institutionalized in Cuba in the 1960s and influenced guerrilla struggles in other parts of the continent. Marxist theories emphasized the need for political mobilization through trade union activism, general strikes and political action led by mass organizations before the onset of armed struggle. Che emphasized the primacy of the foco; that is of the band of revolutionary cadres in generating revolutionary consciousness through armed struggle. Unconventional wars cannot wait, he reiterated for the development of revolutionary consciousness of the mass of the people; neither is it necessary to wait until all conditions for making revolution exist. The guerrilla has to create such consciousness through armed struggle.

At the same time, Che's interpretation of the objective and subjective conditions for revolution marked a sharp departure from orthodox Marxism and prompted sharp criticism from a section of Marxists who subscribed to gradualism for two reasons. First, his revolutionaries did not have to await the maturation of objective conditions, but the primacy given to the political can lead them into blind alleys. Second, since the guerrilla is responsible for leading the war as well as revolutionizing peasant consciousness, Che obliterated the distinction between a communist party and its armed wing. The guerrilla played a military as well as a political role. It is not surprising that the military aspect of the war overrode the political aspect of guerrilla war, or the task of the vanguard party to mobilize collective consciousness.

The problems are manifest. If guerrillas head directly into armed struggle without any serious mobilization of the people, argues Chaliand, they are cut off from popular support. Considering that in the basic political strategy of revolutionary war, factors of time, space and costs are important, the scant taste exhibited in South America for the sense of the long haul on which revolutionary war depends is more than surprising. According to Chaliand, two months before his death Che noted in his diary, regretfully we can presume, that not one peasant had joined the guerrilla group.[17]

Preconditions of people's war

Compare this strategy with that of inviting people into history through imaginative techniques of mobilization. An instance of the latter is provided by the remarkable armed struggle in the Portuguese colony of Guinea Bissau and Cape Verde. The struggle was inspired by one of the most extraordinary thinkers and strategists the world has known – Amilcar Cabral. Compared to China and Vietnam, the case of Guinea Bissau is lesser known. But under the leadership of Cabral a small and poor country in the west coast of Africa was to fight a people's war against Portuguese troops backed by the might of the NATO, drive them to the edge of neuro-physical exhaustion and unilaterally declare independence in 1973. The armed struggle in Guinea Bissau, Mozambique and Angola against Portuguese colonialism catalysed a coup in Lisbon against the military regime in 1974 and brought an end to Portuguese colonialism.

More significantly, Cabral's theory, painstakingly constructed out of a welter of fine empirical detail about lives his people led under Portuguese colonialism, performed after Mao another dramatic U-turn in the Marxist theory of revolution. As a poor primarily agrarian economy, Guinea Bissau lacked an urban proletariat. There was of course the peasantry, but the peasantry, argued Cabral, lacked *prise de conscience*, or political consciousness of its own exploitation.

In 1956, Cabral in association with other radicals set up the PAIGC. Interestingly, the party drew strength from a class that Marx had dismissed contemptuously as the *lumpen* proletariat.

The political significance of this class had been first recognized by Fanon in his theory of urban guerrilla war that broke out in the capital of Algeria, so magnificently captured in Giles Pontecorvo's 1966 *Battle of Algiers*. Cabral was to term this class, composed randomly of beggars, dockworkers, unemployed youth, sex workers and other marginal sections of the urban populations as *de-classe* or outside the class system. At the same time, he concluded that in a society, which neither possessed a working class nor a politicized peasantry, it is this assorted group that could provide the warp and weft of a vanguard party, with cadres reaching into the countryside to construct a political support structure. Cabral and the cadres of the PAIGC patiently worked among the peasants and convinced them that a nationalist as well as a social revolution was indispensable for their well-being.

'Father why is there no chicken on your plate?' This deceptively simple question over a scant lunch provided by the peasant was, but, a prologue to a more detailed discussion of colonial exploitation. Slowly but surely popular support was built up, and the early 1960s armed struggle erupted in the countryside. By 1966, the party had consolidated control over half of the country. At the same time, the PAIGC established alternative political, administrative and economic structures in the liberated regions. Representative institutions took root, and party cadres made special efforts to bring women into these structures. Villagers were trained to manage militias, as well as the organization and supervision of production and distribution.

In liberated zones, the party carefully and patiently constructed participative and democratic institutions and practices, made serious efforts to eliminate constraints on women, established organizations to disburse health and education and replaced the commodification of agricultural products by the barter system. Through these processes, the party created and nurtured a close connection between the guerrillas and their constituency. The dual strategy of building up popular support as a prelude to the launch of war, and constructing institutions in liberated zones, impacted both the colonized and the colonizer. The latter initiated countermeasures in order to improve the material conditions of the peasantry and neutralize the revolution. The colonial state also instituted strategies to encourage identity politics and divide the people on ethnic lines. Yet the PAIGC managed to successfully undermine these strategies and the colonial army, and won some notable victories.

The political visionary Amilcar Cabral was assassinated on 20 January 1973, about eight months before the declaration of independence. His death dealt a grievous blow to the struggle, but the party continued to tread the path he had patiently carved out of a daunting social landscape. General elections were held to the People's National Assembly in the liberated zones. The party also launched a diplomatic offensive in order to convert other countries to its cause and organized party congresses. In 1974, the 1973 unilateral declaration of independence was recognized by Portugal, and Guinea Bissau and Cape Verde became independent.

A backward, agricultural country had launched war on a colonial power that was supported by the mighty forces of NATO and won a political victory! The achievement was nothing short of stunning and bore witness to the success of the line of people's war. Interestingly, Cabral did not at any point of time admit that he was a Marxist or a Maoist. His strategy emerged out of detailed empirical study of the possibilities and the potentials of an underdeveloped peasant society.[18] That his technique reflected that of Mao Zedong who had tailored the theory and strategy of revolutionary war to the specific conditions of China is manifest.

Two models of guerrilla war are at hand. The first model is prevalent in South America. Here warfare, which has been influenced heavily by the Foco theory, has had little success, mainly because the leaders have not differentiated between the military and the political arm of the party. The military aspects of the war are not, in sum, controlled by the political. In the case of Guinea Bissau, China and Vietnam, revolutionary movements have been simultaneously national and social. In these cases, the party saw wide-ranging political mobilization as an essential precondition of revolutionary war.

The primacy of the political

Specific to the Maoist theory of guerrilla war is the notion of a people's war. The decisive factor in armed struggle Mao theorized is not weapons but people who are convinced of the rightness of a cause. 'Without a political goal, guerrilla warfare must fail, as it must, if its political objectives do not coincide with the aspirations of the people and their sympathy, co-operation and assistance cannot be gained. The essence of guerrilla warfare is thus revolutionary in character.'[19] Guerrilla operations are not an independent form of warfare; they are one step in the total war, one aspect of the revolutionary struggle.

The recognition that guerrilla war in the radical mode will simply not work unless a highly organized political party is linked to the people was the particular contribution of Mao and later Cabral, among others, to theories of revolution. Of importance is the recognition that popular consciousness, catalyzed by the vanguard of the party, aspires towards not only the abstract goal of liberation, but also to the establishment of concrete institutions and practices that make liberation possible. Under the leadership of the vanguard, villagers who extended support to the guerrilla army in China and Guinea Bissau, in Vietnam and in Mozambique realized that it was possible to create a society free of the debilitating hold of oppressive power. In the process, political consciousness was transformed, and the subjects of a history not their own became agents of a history that they would make with the harnessing of energies and political passions to the project.

Let us in light of these considerations begin to enquire into the nature of politics espoused by the Maoists in India who subscribe to the objective of peoples' war, and who believe that the political mobilization of the constituency is of prime significance. Political mobilization can, arguably, be seen in two ways. In a pejorative sense, we can dismiss political mobilization as indoctrination or as rhetoric and propaganda designed to turn public opinion in precisely *this* particular direction and in no other. The other sense in which we can think of political mobilization is as a catalyst, or a facilitator. In this sense, the strategy assumes that people, howsoever ordinary be the lives they lead, possess the capacity to make practical judgements and to make sense of the lives they live.

The Italian Marxist Antonio Gramsci (1891–1937) called this intrinsic human capacity common sense. Common sense in the Gramscian vision indicates that each individual holds a certain set of beliefs, which may well be unreflective, spontaneous, incoherent and even contradictory. What is significant is that these belief patterns give to the holder a certain idea of what the world is about, and how to judge it.

For Gramsci, all people, and not just scholars trained in academic departments of universities, are philosophers. They possess beliefs that help them make sense of the world. These beliefs are composed of notions and concepts, common sense and good sense and popular religion. After having shown that every person is a philosopher in so far as she or he possesses a specific conception of the world, Gramsci tells us to move in a second direction, that of awareness and criticism. Should we, he asks, think without critical awareness in a disjointed and episodic way? Or, is it better to work out consciously and critically one's own conception of the world?[20]

The second question enables us to understand the limits of popular psyches. In most cases, 'good sense' tends to mesh and inextricably so with superstition, folklore and religious understanding. What we call common sense, or the way we see the world, is dominated by the ideas of the ruling class. These classes, according to Gramsci, present their particular interests and worldviews as universal and proceed to disseminate this 'trick' through social, political, economic and cultural institutions and practices in civil society. The strategy is enormously effective, and people begin to believe that this is how things are, and this is how the world works; it does not, it simply cannot, work in any other way. The generation of consent through practices of everyday life, cultural institutions and pedagogy Gramsci called hegemony.

Thereupon the specific task of intellectuals and activists, wrote Gramsci, is not to dismiss pervasive beliefs as cases of mere 'false consciousness'. The task of the revolutionary is to engage with the chaotic aggregate of disparate conceptions that add up to common sense. The intellectual and the activist have to patiently work towards dismantling the old and instilling in its place new beliefs, a new common sense, a new culture and a new philosophy that allows people to articulate a critical and an alternative world view.

In sum, Gramsci tells us that the intellectual, the activist and vanguard cadres have to accept that all persons possess common sense. This is a given. They have to work with and within popular attitudes, but they also have to prise open and dismantle processes that normalize inequality and exploitation, injustice and denial of humanity. It is only then that they can go beyond common sense to create critical ways of thinking about the world. The interior world of individuals and groups has to be thoroughly shaken up; they have to be persuaded to realize that things do not have to be quite this way, and that they can be changed. Political mobilization requires hard work. This is integral to any project of revolutionary transformation.

The theory of people's war goes further than this and insists that along with armed struggle it is necessary to build popular support structures and to establish alternative institutions and practices in liberated areas. These alternative institutions can be seen as the nucleus of a future state. Alternative ways of thinking, practices and institutions introduce the constituency to the possibilities of politics or prospect of another world without hierarchy, exclusions and injustice. Revolutionary violence as a form of politics holds aloft the idea of politics in the transformative mode. It follows that the more mobilized a population is for warfare, the more revolutionary the outcome will be.

In order to foreground awareness of the political and symbolic economy of injustice, and the pressing need for justice, revolutionaries have the task of explaining to people what the war is for, what the stakes are, what each person is entitled to, what the pitfalls are and why such war has to be waged at all. Above all, they have to communicate their vision of a future society. It is only then that they can carry public opinion along with them.

Popular support is politically significant for people must be convinced of the rightness of a cause. But the need for popular support is also strategic. Unconventional war demands that the guerrilla army skilled at advancing when the enemy retreats, and retreating when it advances, finds ready sanctuary in hamlets and villages and is assured of access to food, shelter and information. Above all, political mobilization is essential. Whereas violence propels the recovery of agency, reliance on violence alone, as Fanon told us, can prove deceptive. The long forked tongue of violence poisons everything from the psyche of the victim to the psyche of those who think they have been liberated. Violence possesses an uncanny ability to reproduce itself in new guises: today in the persona of the colonizer, tomorrow in the persona of the new political elite. In order to prove genuinely liberating, this form of politics should be yoked to a project that seeks to overturn existing injustices. Political mobilization has to precede actual fighting. In short, violence has to be controlled by politics and subordinated to political mobilization and to the realization of political visions. These are the principles that can help us to evaluate the armed struggle in the heartland of Maoism. They are not external to the ideology and the strategy of Maoism; these principles stem from the political philosophy of revolutionary violence – the primacy of politics.

The case of India: The primacy of violence

In the 1980s, cadres of Peoples War Group were hounded out of the state of Andhra Pradesh by state-sponsored irregular forces called the Greyhounds. Intent on escape, the cadres entered the Dandakaranya forest region. Here they began to organize the villagers to claim rights over land, resources and forest produce. In the process, they garnered support from the tribals. The party established front organizations and membership of these organizations, such as the peasant–worker front and the womens' front swelled considerably.

It is not as if the people among whom the Maoists came to work, and on whose behalf they picked up the gun, lacked political consciousness. Peasant and tribal rebellions have been an integral part of the history and folklore of central India. What the Maoists have done is to integrate memories of and revolts against oppression into a broader vision that is ideologically informed and historically grounded. This is an essential part of political mobilization. Yet when it comes to the question of whether the Maoists have followed the script authored by theories, practices and the history of people's war, we run into a raging controversy. The jury is still out on this question. On balance, even sympathizers of the Maoists are forced to accept that the struggle is more military than political for reasons that are not difficult to fathom.

Normally, guerrillas set out to cultivate popular support through political education and transmission of a political vision through various modes of visual and oral representation. An unconventional peoples' war cannot be run on coercion alone. At the minimum, cadres of the party have to excite a certain amount of popular sympathy for the cause and for war. In regions in central and eastern India, the Maoists began to disseminate a vision of a future unshackled from bonds of caste and class, through village meetings, community groups, theatre performances, speeches, public meetings and lectures in schools. In pursuit of a just order, they fought for higher wages, redistributed land and charted out agrarian strategies.

Yet scholars and activists who have done fieldwork in Maoist areas tell us that in Bastar, Jharkand and parts of Andhra Pradesh, the Maoists employ tremendous coercion to bring the constituency to heel. Kangaroo courts sentence suspected informers, landowners, moneylenders, errant revenue officials, delinquent party members, school teachers and government officials to brutal punishment and certain death by slitting the throat of the offender. Can this be accounted for as collateral damage, or as the costs ordinary people have to pay for revolutions?

Moreover, the reported participation of the Maoists in corruption, whether pricing of tendu leaves, or taking a cut from the contractors or imposing taxes on infrastructure projects, has deeply compromised the political dream of building an alternative to the system that exists. Alpha Shah's argument that the Maoists run protection rackets in Jharkand has dented the image of our flaming revolutionaries to quite an extent.[21]

Armed cadres have of course the power of coercing local populations into supporting them and their ideology and dispensing with political mobilization. They have guns; the villagers do not. But if the objective of revolutionary war is to liberate people whose lives have been since birth yoked to threefold disadvantage, and if the intention is to create a new society based on redistribution of material resources and recognition of equal worth, this strategy will necessarily prove not only counterproductive but also subversive of the basic tenets of revolutionary war.

Violence without politics

From the perspective of peoples' war, the indiscriminate use of coercion to herd people to the fold of Maoism runs up a number of problems. First, it catapults an issue that many are familiar with, and many are unfamiliar with; that people who lead the armed struggle need not be the people who are subjected to triple injustice, to the centre of the political stage. We simply do not know whether the tribals and the Scheduled Castes in the Red Corridor have been persuaded, coaxed or coerced into sharing the goals of the party. Neither do we know whether they prefer immediate solutions to pressing problems, compared to the long-term objectives of seizing state power. It is also debatable whether villagers line up behind cadres of the party out of fear, or whether they are genuine converts to the ideology of the party. Is the party characterized by the use of force rather than mobilization? Reports from the field suggest that the former is more prevalent.

Ironically, suggests Bela Bhatia who has carried out fieldwork in Bihar and Andhra Pradesh, a movement that promises liberation can actually land up making people feel less free. It is also problematic that members of mass fronts pay the price for actions taken by the underground party. These actions, again ironically, are taken on behalf of the people but without their knowledge or consent. The use of violence has taken a heavy toll, she concludes.[22]

Second, we can hardly overlook the political context of democracy in which the Maoists have launched armed struggle. No village in times of competitive democracy and an even more competitive market economy can remain a political *tabula rasa* or a neutral site into which an armed group can march and proceed to persuade, influence and rouse people to action. It is doubtful whether any social collective in history has ever been without tensions and rivalries, but competitive electoral democracy creates its own schisms. Resultantly, each village is earmarked by complex pecking orders, competing structures of loyalty to 'this' leader or 'that' political party, feuds large and small, with each group wishing to score points off another, and modes of garnering profit through informal economies.

Guerrillas might use villagers instrumentally to secure shelter, food and information. Villagers can also use a man with a gun instrumentally; this might help them to settle disputes. These complexities make the task of sorting out the issue whether this is a people's war; a war conceived and executed by elites, or a war that serves the interest of some group or the other, a difficult one.

Third, if the use of coercion to harvest and retain support inhibits the task of political mobilization, the task is further truncated by the tremendous coercion deployed by the state. In response to the guerrilla war launched by the Maoists, the Indian state has marshalled formidable military arsenals, mounted a military onslaught on the region termed the 'Red Corridor' and surrounded guerrilla zones. Counter-insurgency doctrines learnt from guerrilla struggles and the war against terrorism have given to security forces strategic advantage. The consequences are serious, for the military offensive launched by the Indian state against the Maoists has forced the guerrilla militia to concentrate energies on rearguard action and protect fields of operation. That this strategy has come at the expense of the political component of the peoples' war doctrine is manifest. The ultimate objective of launching a people's war to overturn existing forms of power, and to create a people's democracy, has been pre-empted if not aborted by the onslaught of the security forces.

Both time and space for intense, sustained and prolonged political mobilization is denied to the Maoists. When the energies of the armed wings of the party are focussed on defending their regions of engagement, opportunities for unremitting political mobilization through dissemination of ideology and the harnessing of energies to a cause cannot, but, be scarce. The Maoists, as Barnard D'Mello, a keen observer of party strategy, points out, have not succeeded in turning any of the guerrilla zones into base areas where they can establish a miniature state based on self-reliant economic development and land to the tiller.[23] If that is so, the one factor that makes radical armed struggle acceptable, notably that cadres introduce people into alternative ways of doing things, whether production or regulation of social relations, and the belief that these alternative ways will enhance agency, is greatly subverted.

Fourth, if the Maoists seem to have underestimated the military power of the Indian state, they also seem to have underestimated the legitimacy that Indian democracy, howsoever flawed be that democracy, commands, even among people who continue to be triply disadvantaged. Sumanta Bannerjee suggests that in India, a parliamentary republic, despite large-scale corruption and criminality, still enjoys democratic legitimacy among wide sections of the people, and major contending social groups find democracy useful for their own ends. 'The system apparently has not yet exhausted all its potentialities of exploiting the hopes and aspirations of the Indian poor and underprivileged sections.'[24] The sophisticated bourgeois Indian state, skilled in evoking and harnessing loyalties to its own cause, is even more skilled in neutralizing challenges and upping the ante.

The state has taken the initiative to introduce a number of measures designed to reverse legacies of underdevelopment, ameliorate poverty that was fuelling the conflict and embark on development. Bureaucrats now concentrate energies on the most neglected districts in which armed struggle prevails, try to establish secure access to education, organize camps on preventive and curative health care, repair infrastructure and improve the distribution of food grains. The central government has given financial support to the state governments for the purpose of instituting long-term development projects as well as provision of social goods. In sum, the 'clear, hold, and develop' strategy uses the 'magic mantra' of development to win back tribal populations.

After decades of neglect, the government has now taken up projects such as constructing infrastructure, particularly landmine proof, roller compacted concrete roads in Maoist zones, under the protection of the combat forces of the Central Reserve Police Force. The parallel with Fidel Castro, who built modern highways in the Sierra Maestra region of Cuba to reward inhabitants for their support but also to ensure that guerrilla onslaughts would not be repeated, is striking. The history of guerrilla war highlights the importance of remote and difficult terrains. Modern means of communication and information technology have managed to neutralize the potential of guerrilla war to fight an army that is technologically superior in many ways.

Achievements of Maoism: The irony

We, of course, cannot say that nothing has been done by our revolutionaries. Whereas the long-term goal of the Maoists is the takeover of state power, their immediate objective is to carry out land reform, construct irrigation projects to protect the villagers from drought, protect peasants against moneylenders, fight atrocities on the lower castes and launch struggles against mining corporates intent on displacing villagers from land. Analysts and field reports tell us that in some regions land has been transferred to the tiller, aid extended to poor farmers, cooperatives set up, measures to obtain just prices for agricultural commodities and minor forest produce put in place, modern knowledge about agriculture disseminated, better quality seeds gathered from elsewhere have been distributed and voluntary labour to construct tanks with canal systems deployed.[25]

Will this go a long way in building up popular support for the cause? Do measures initiated by the Maoists provide the sort of alternative structures that were put in place in liberated zones in Vietnam, China and Guinea Bissau, alternative both to feudal structures of exploitation and the many injustices of capitalism?

Nirmalangshu Mukherji has made an interesting point in this context. Even if wages in the region have increased because of the bargains the Maoists have finalized with the contractors, he suggests, these are far less than the minimum wages paid in other parts of the country, for example Kerala.[26] The irony is that the initiatives taken by the Maoists appear but a pale resemblance of development projects in other parts of the country, projects initiated by the same state they wish to overthrow. Nandini Sundar makes roughly the same point. The Maoists have established mass organizations in Dandakaranya guerrilla zone and carried out development work. But, these initiatives simply cannot match what the government could have done for the villagers, if only it had the political will to do so.[27]

Far from providing alternative modes of social and economic relationships, the Maoist development agenda seems to have become a mirror image of dominant worldviews, doppelgangers no more. This is an ironic reversal of revolutionary imaginaries. Compared to the development models established in the rest of the country, these strategies of agricultural development are at best routine and primitive. Thirty years of occupation of a backward region has neither resulted in the establishment of alternative development models, nor in the construction of schools and hospitals that might have lessened illiteracy and ill health. The inhabitants of these regions continue to be severely malnourished, and high levels of infant mortality and illiteracy mark the area. The cadres of the party could have formed democratically constituted cooperatives to administer livelihoods in tribal-controlled panchayats, collected and delivered tendu leaves and eliminated contractors.[28] But, they chose to go the way of mainstream development.

What is it, then, that the Maoists have accomplished even as they have let loose violence in pursuit of a radically new society, and even as this violence has catalysed extreme violence by the state? John Harriss holds that the Maoists have tapped into and to some extent, at least, have articulated the long-standing grievances of Dalits and landless peasants against high-caste landowners and the grievances of the tribal people against the state for what it has done, notably displacement and sanctioning of repressive policies, as well as what it has not done, that is provision of basic necessities.[29]

What has the revolution accomplished?

Indisputably, revolutionaries dramatically foregrounded the interests of the poorest of the poor, an agenda that had been washed off the economic success story that countries in the global south have written for themselves. Yet the use of violence to focalize ill-being casts a sorry reflection not only on the inability of the state to provide for needy citizens, but also on the political worldview of revolutionaries. Do democratic governments come alive to the needs of the triply oppressed only when they take recourse to violence or back those who employ violence? Has revolutionary violence in India become the harbinger of a world that is not significantly different from what exists in other parts of the country?

Revolution is justified when people have been denied what is their due according to the creed of democratic justice – an equal share in the burdens and benefits of society. Injustice has to be reversed, and people who have suffered under triple disadvantage have to be assured that they will participate equally in sharing the benefits and burdens of society. Instead democratic states come to them as a bearer of rewards if they were only to shun the revolutionaries and threats of coercion if they fail to do so. And the Maoists do what a bourgeois democratic state should have done for its own people. They too promise rewards and threaten coercion in case people do not support them.

In order to placate discontent and delegitimize the Maoist agenda, the government has undertaken development. Yet these measures concentrate on either one or a cluster of immediate issues, leaving the big issues untouched – huge social inequalities, skewed landholding patterns, the dominance of corporate capitalism, greed of industrialists for more mineral-rich land irrespective of consequences and the tremendous poverty that stalks the steps of large numbers of Indians. Where there is inequality, there must be unfreedom. But, the state simply does not tackle the source of powerlessness and helplessness, offshoots of triple disadvantage. Its response to the armed struggle is piecemeal and partial. Along with threats of coercion, piecemeal practices – building of a school here and building of a clinic there – strengthen the hold of the state over its people. It turns citizens into consumers. What then of justice? Development cannot provide justice; it may even exacerbate injustice in other forms, pace displacement?

If the objective of revolutionary violence is to reshape the political context in which we live, then we need a politics that has an infinitely broader vision than that replicating the development project of the state: that little bit more income, a little bit more land, a little bit more control over one's own life. Revolutionary politics demands that people be brought into a relationship of solidarity with each other, that inequalities be seriously tackled, and that citizens participate in the constitution of a public and critical discourse, where each participant is heard with equal respect.

We have to ask this question with some regret. Are the Maoists fighting a people's war at great cost to themselves and to their constituency only to implement the agenda of mainstream parties? Tilak Gupta has put the point across well, to tell the truth, he writes, there is not much of a difference between the Maoist programme and that of communist parties functioning within the system of parliamentary democracy. The correspondence between clauses relating to land reforms, fair wages for labour, recognition of the right to work as a fundamental right, improvement of farming methods, removal of gender discrimination in matters of wages and ownership of land and promotion of peasant cooperatives is striking. It is true that no political party has followed the cause of the rural poor with so much zeal. The Maoists have tried to fill this vacuum. But they are more eager to propagate the path of armed revolution than to pursue revolutionary aims.[30] The diminution of the Maoist agenda has become painfully apparent. Can people who have been rendered voiceless under the burden of triple injustice regain agency?

Moreover, when the central and the state government of the 'affected areas' delivers to the people social and economic political goods, is not the immediate agenda of the Maoists rendered redundant? History bears witness to this. Sumanta Banerjee tells us that in Naxalbari, the rural poor who joined the armed Maoist insurrection have today dropped out of from the movement and accepted instead economic benefits, such as a small piece of cultivable land, higher wages for labour and participation in decision-making offered to them by the parliamentary Left. While travelling in the Bengal countryside, he writes, 'I listen to a new generation of rural people who nurture dreams of a better future within this system rather than change it through an armed revolution'.[31]

When it comes to converting people into stakeholders in the system, no institution works as well as that of private property. Private property dissolves radicalism and fosters the status quo. It is this very strategy which is being used by the government to divide poor and landless peasant from each other, and from those who would fight their cause.

Political violence without the political

The main problem, it seems to me, is another one. Given the context of a democracy that is considered legitimate by many, and given the military might of the Indian state, the space and time for political mobilization of the constituency of the Maoists has shrunk dramatically. Without the political in the concept of political violence, we are left with violence. Fanon had warned us that though anger, rage and revenge lead to violence, these sentiments are not enough to liberate people. Spontaneous and passionate outbursts of violence will disintegrate if the users of violence do not graduate to a different level of political consciousness. A transformative agenda can be created only when people seek horizons hitherto undreamt of, beyond the reach of violence. Otherwise, the political elite will do little except reproduce the violence of the order.

When Charu Majumdar called for annihilation of the class enemy in the first phase of Naxalism, his idea was not only to challenge a system that had consigned people to penury, but also to reinvent a new self in direct opposition to a subjugated and passive self of the pre-violence days. The problem is that without politics in command, violence goes berserk. It can best be likened to a quagmire that relentlessly sucks people into its murky depths. From here there is no escape. When violence holds individuals and groups in thrall, moral disintegration follows. For we cannot control violence, violence controls us. Fanon had told us long ago that when the colonial finger writes the alphabet of power in blood and gore, the script is ineffaceable and the imprint it leaves on the body politic, indelible. Violence leaves stigmata much like the murder of Duncan left blood on Lady Macbeth's hands: 'What, will these hands ne'er be clean?' How can, then, a new society free of oppression and exploitation be created? All we will have on our hands is a blood-stained history, not a political history that can show the way out of the highly exploitative society that we have on our hands today.

If revolutionary violence is about politics more than violence, then Maoism has to be judged in terms of whether it has managed to (a) go beyond Gramscian common sense and introduce people to critical perspectives on and engagement with Indian society (b) set in place alternative institutions and practices that introduce beleaguered communities to the wider goal of the armed struggle, an alternative society, economy and politics (c) enabled ordinary people to realize agency. Political mobilization serves to catalyse political consciousness and encourage people to stand up and be counted as actors in their own right. This is the basic criterion on which we judge the efficacy of political practices. Indisputably the project of Maoism is geared towards all these objectives.

Yet the political and the military context proscribes sustained political mobilization of people caught up in the trap of triple injustice. Politically, the Indian state despite the many injustices it perpetrates is seen as legitimate in the eyes of the citizens, largely because it is democratic. The village is thus not a neutral site, receptive to political mobilization in the radical mode. The village is apt to be divided and fragmented between those who back the state and those who back the Maoist agenda. The outbreak of armed struggle has compelled the Indian state to introduce and accelerate development initiatives in zones of conflict. The Indian state has also launched a major military onslaught against Maoist strongholds. Caught between the Scylla of massive military operations and the Charybdis of state-led development initiatives, the Maoists are denied both time and space in which they can engage in sustained mobilization and establish institutions that code a radically different perspective.

Whereas a people's war is more about politics than coercion, and more about political visions mediating the course of armed struggle, things seem to be different in the case of Maoism. The use of violence against class enemies and against the state not only leads to loss of lives but also to fear. We do not know whether people line up behind the Maoists out of fear or out of conviction. Whether agency can be realized in an environment where the guerrilla forces are engaged in a rearguard action against the might of the Indian state, and when the constituency is terrorized by the same weapons used to fight the state, the political agenda is put by the wayside. This is incontrovertible. No politics that focuses on telling people what they are owed by society can succeed when the environment is stamped by violence. Moreover, whatever alternative institutions have been built by the Maoists, observers tell us that these are mirror images of dominant development agendas. In sum, the Maoist agenda is diminished because it has unfolded in a context very different to the colonial context in which guerrilla wars proved successful. Revolutionary violence without revolutionary politics further truncates the agenda. And, the case for justifying revolutionary violence because it enables agency is deeply compromised.

Conclusion

Political violence without political mobilization, for all seeming heroism and daredevilry, is a lazy way of doing politics. It is executed by a handful of cadres, and it eschews transformation of either the body politic or of its members. Violence as spectacle reduces people into an audience or bystanders. In the process, nothing changes, perhaps nothing ever could, not even the recovery of agency.

In sum, we have to be aware of the indeterminacy and the unpredictability of this avatar of politics, and the incapacity of human beings to control violence, or rather the relentless impulse of violence to control those who handle it for definable ends. Any study of revolutionary violence has to track the dilemmas, the quandaries and the political predicaments that stalk the practice of revolutionary violence. This is the lesson from history. The lesson from history and from an investigation into the practice of revolutionary politics is outlined in the conclusion.

Conclusion

Political practices tend to be untidy, unruly and contradictory. Revolutionary politics is definitely untidier, certainly more unruly and without doubt more contradictory than other forms of politics. These characteristics defy neat theorization, systematic conceptualization and unambiguous conclusions. If we try to fit complex and inconsistent practices into conceptual straightjackets and then label these uncompromisingly as 'good' or 'bad', we will simply miss out the paradox of revolutionary politics in democracies. The paradox is as follows. Even if we subscribe to the objectives of revolutionary violence, even if we understand the reason for the eruption of violence in democratic contexts, we can still believe that revolutionary violence is politically unwise or imprudent.

In order to demonstrate this contradiction, I make two distinct arguments in this work. Revolutionary violence can be justified. Revolutionary politics in democratic contexts is politically imprudent. How do we make up our minds on the issue? Before we proceed on that route, let me lay down the four propositions that are derived from this study.

Proposition I: Significance of the political context

Revolutionary violence does not permit of a general defence the way we would defend say the right to dissent or the right to civil disobedience. Any justification of political or revolutionary violence has to be contextual. This is true of the generic concept of violence as well. Take the case of a woman subjected to domestic abuse day after day, night after night. If one day this woman picks up a frying pan of boiling oil and pours it on the head of her errant spouse, will we judge her in quite the same way we judge her spouse who intentionally tortures her? Criminal law recognizes extenuating circumstances, or the specificity of the context for the eruption of violence, even if judges fervently believe that violence is an unmitigated bad.

Accordingly, the argument in this work suggests that in certain and specified circumstances revolutionary violence lends itself to prima facie justification. That is the justification of revolutionary violence is context-dependent. For example, thousands of people in parts of India, now labelled the 'Red Corridor', suffer from triple injustice that is highly resistant to any sort of change. We can easily side with the argument that the only way of emancipating the poorest of the poor – the most discriminated against and those who lack voice in the public domain – from conditions that impair them is to smash the system through the use of violence. Violence becomes a weapon of the last resort in such cases. More significantly, revolutionary violence is intended to act as a catalyst in the transition to a less exploitative society and to give through struggle agency to the oppressed. This is the chief legitimacy claim of revolutionary violence, a claim that distinguishes it from other forms of political violence.

Notably, revolutionary politics is justified not only because people suffer extreme deprivation and social discrimination, but because democracy has either left unfulfilled or infringed its basic presupposition – democratic justice. The principle of democratic justice rules that no person will be deprived of an equal share of the benefits of a society. And no person shall have to shoulder more than her fair share of the burdens of society. If this norm of justice, which reflects and codifies the basic presupposition of democracy, equality, is infringed, the resort to revolutionary violence by affected groups can be justified.

Proposition Ib: Significance of the political context

If revolutionary violence is justified only by reference to the context, whether this form of politics will or will not succeed is also context-dependent. For example, history teaches us that revolutionary guerrilla wars have won spectacular victories against colonialism. Whether it was the liberation war in Algeria, the first Indo-China war, Guinea Bissau, Mozambique, Angola, Vietnam and China, guerrilla wars succeeded in mobilizing masses to their cause, secured support and won notable political victories. In all these struggles, the class project that was inspired by revolutionary Maoist ideology was part of a national anti-colonial struggle.

For example, Amilcar Cabral laid great stress on the development of revolutionary consciousness and on the institutionalization of alternative value systems in liberated zones. But for him the main contradiction was that between the colony and the colonizer. Revolution for Cabral meant the right of every people to have their own history, and the right to free national productive forces from colonial fetters.[1] The movement for liberation, arguably, fetched a mass following because the struggle had a national and not only a class dimension. In other cases too, it was nationalism/anti-colonialism that succeeded in sparking off political imaginations, and converting people to the cause of independence, than only the class struggle.

Consider China known for having fashioned a revolution that prioritized the peasant rather than the worker and guerrilla struggle rather than trade union action in urbanized and industrialized countries. In 1962, Chalmers Johnson who taught Chinese and Japanese politics at Berkeley and at San Diego Universities published his acclaimed work on *Peasant Nationalism and Communist Power: The Emergence of Revolutionary China, 1937–1945*. Drawing on archives of secret Japanese wartime material that he had collected for his doctoral supervisor, Johnson controversially claimed that the mobilization of millions of peasants was made possible because the Chinese people, fired by nationalist fervour, were determined to resist the Japanese invasion in North China. The communist rise to power in China, argued Johnson, was a species of a nationalist movement. The movement from 1935 onwards concentrated on national salvation more than land distribution and class war.[2]

If nationalism rather than class war has been the dominant reason for the success of revolutionary wars in colonial contexts, then the prospect of a successful class war in a society that is independent, democratic and seen as legitimate by even the constituency of the revolutionaries is remote. Pessimism on this front is not unwarranted.

Revolutionaries face a much more formidable enemy than colonialism in the democratic state, even if the norms of justice have been imperfectly institutionalized in this state. Even if political equality is attended by social and economic inequality, even if political equality does not give to people equal 'voice' as distinguished from an equal 'vote', the idea that we can elect and dismiss governments is a seductive one. The *idea* of democracy is seldom matched by the institutionalization of democracy. But it is precisely the power of this *idea* that has moved millions to protest and motivated others to vest confidence in democratic institutions and in the constitution. The more critically inclined may carp and complain about imperfectly just democracies, but we cannot deny that electoral democracy possesses its own unique charm. It gives hope that at some time things will become better. Perhaps the government may listen to the voices of the disprivileged, perhaps civil society groups may take up their cause, perhaps elected representatives will become less insensitive and more responsive and accountable and perhaps the rest of society will be liberated from selfish and narrow preoccupations with the self and begin to think about the well-being of fellow citizens.

Not surprisingly, in democracies, political mobilization by revolutionaries turns into a contest between existing loyalties to power holders and evoking loyalties to a cause weighted in favour of the poorest and the most exploited. It is not clear which way the tide will turn because as in the case of India, though the state is coercive, the Maoists have also displayed remarkable inclination to coercion. If the Maoists struggle for social and economic justice, the Indian state is also the dispenser of largesse. When it comes to winning hearts and minds a democratic state, undeniably, commands infinitely more symbolic and material resources than our revolutionaries. The

Maoists have appropriated land from landlords, vide kangaroo courts, and redistributed it to peasant who had worked on other's land for generations in return for a pittance. But when the state gets into the act, it gives to the landless legal title to land. Private property has its uses; it converts the constituency of revolution into landlords of small- or medium-size landholdings. And proprietors of land have a stake in upholding the establishment. History bears witness to this. Sumanta Banerjee tells us that in Naxalbari, the rural poor who joined the armed Maoist insurrection have today dropped out of the movement and accepted economic benefits, such as a small piece of cultivable land, higher wages for labour and participation in decision-making offered to them by the parliamentary Left. While travelling in the Bengal countryside, he writes, 'I listen to a new generation of rural people who nurture dreams of a better future within this system rather than change it through an armed revolution.'[3]

When it comes to converting people into stakeholders in the system, no institution works as well as that of private property. Private property dissolves radicalism and fosters the status quo. It is this very strategy which is being used by the government to divide poor and landless peasant from each other and from those who would fight their cause. There is after all no section of society that is politically more conservative than those who own private property.

If constituencies are so easily won over by sops such as ownership of small pieces of land, the vanguard party has obviously failed to politicize popular consciousness in the direction of revolutionary consciousness which passionately desires a new society. Unless the use of violence is subordinated to the political cause of revolutionizing consciousness, the peasant will tend to choose the softer option. Why should she not? Assured land rights are much more tangible and secure than a life of Hobbesian uncertainty.

Ultimately, it is for the villagers to decide which way they want to go. But if they have to decide which way they want to go, or which path will lead to the recovery of agency, the political context has to be free of violence both of the state and of the Maoists. No one can make choices in a context that is shaped on all sides by one sort of violence or another. Violence is simply not conducive to the recovery of agency. Both the democratic state and our revolutionaries deny to people who have been stripped of agency the appropriate political context in which they can choose how they want to make their own history.

In sum, colonial powers deployed awesome military power against nationalist guerrilla war, but in country after country, the revolutionaries won notable political victories. Revolutionary wars against independent democratic governments have never quite succeeded in their objective. In Nepal, the Maoists gave up their weapons and joined the electoral process. In India, the struggle of the Maoists has continued in one form or the other and in one state or the other. They have not given up, but they have also not been able to secure liberated zones.

The democratic state has also shown itself capable of inflicting awesome violence to repress any sign of insurrection. Revolutionary forces, as suggested in the previous chapter, have to focus on mere survival against the onslaught of a militarized state. Where is then the space or the time for political mobilization of the constituency? Certainly, the suppressed recover voice and acquire agency when they pick up the gun and confront the oppressor. There is probably nothing as heady as confronting the oppressor with a weapon in one's hand. Fanon had, however, warned us that unless violence is harnessed to a political project of liberation, the revolutionary momentum of the war will be lost. It will just peter out.

The two propositions offered above focus on the importance of political contexts in justifying revolutionary politics and also point out the difficulties confronted by this form of politics. Revolutionary violence is justified by the context or the circumstances in which people are forced to live stark and bare lives. In such circumstances, revolutionary violence becomes a weapon of the last resort, as well as a scalpel that cuts through the strong threads that bind multiple injustices together. Considering the sort of lives that people live in the region termed the 'Red Corridor' in India, we have few defences against the argument for revolutionary violence. The context in this case justifies the text.

The second proposition holds that the larger political context whether of colonialism or of independent democratic states will greatly influences the outcome of revolutionary violence. In colonial contexts, the enemy is clear, an alien power that has taken away from the people of the territory the right to self-rule. Anti-colonial guerrilla wars had a strong nationalist component, and it is not unfeasible that people clustered around the movement not by reasons of class but by reasons of anti-imperialism.

In independent and democratic countries, the chances of success of revolutionary politics become much more difficult. Mobilization by the revolutionaries can be outmatched by the democratic state employing all the resources as its command to 'win hearts and minds'. The outbreak of violence is also outmatched by the democratic state employing deadly weapons against its own citizens. Democratic governments have succeeded in legitimizing torture, illegal detentions, encounter deaths and imposition of draconian laws that take away civil liberties by reference to national unity and security. Again, it is the notion of the 'national' that helps in consolidating public opinion against revolutionaries. In turn, revolutionaries confronted by the legitimating strategies of a democratic state and intense coercion have to focus energies on guarding their flanks. The net outcome is that we have on our hands violence without politics or rather political mobilization of the constituency that will give to dispossessed people awareness of injustice, the need to break inflexible bonds of oppression through violence and the need for a new society that does not tolerate injustice and that respects the dignity of all. If revolutionaries have few chances in a democracy to pursue the agenda of political awareness and mobilization, both of which give to the dispossessed voice, we have on our hands a peculiar phenomenon – violence as theatre. To put the point across starkly, democratic states are not the best contexts in which to pursue a revolutionary agenda. In democratic countries, we find the phenomenon of revolutions sans politics. This leaves only violence, which converts people into consumers rather than citizens who have recovered voice through struggle.

Proposition II: Violence without politics

Without politics in command, violence not only goes berserk, it reduces prospects that the marginalized will be able to confront an unjust system in a sustained manner, or that they will be able to stand up and speak back to history. The mandate of revolutionary violence is not only violence, the mandate is to transform society and to show the way to a better one, in which little babies will not die of neglect and in which people will not be diminished because the preconditions of a life of dignity have been denied to them. But without sustained mobilization, we get only violence. What we do not get is revolutionary politics that can transform entire societies. Without an agenda of transformative politics, violence misplaces its chief legitimacy claim and becomes a spectator sport.[4] It is just a bad way of doing politics because it subjects people to violence but does not enable them to exercise agency.

More significantly, without revolutionary mobilization, spectacular acts of violence reduce people into an audience and to bystanders. And revolutionary violence is transmuted into a theatre of the absurd. Extravagant acts of political violence may appear courageous, praiseworthy, ruptural and harbingers of change, but they belong to the realm of illusion. For nothing has changed, nothing ever could. Masses might admire and acclaim militants for personal bravery, but they remain untouched and steeped in political passivity. Revolutionary agents lack the capacity to invite them into history or call upon them to make their own history. The people are condemned to remain spectators of actions performed by others and condemned to live out their lives as subjects, not agents.

And those who become rulers will have blood on their hands, blood that does not wash away quite so easily. This is the lesson we learn from the French Revolution. What were the gains of the French

Revolution of 1789 asks the historian Simon Schama rhetorically in his magisterial *Citizens*? If one had to look for one indisputable story of transformation in the French Revolution, it would be the creation of the juridical entity of the citizen. But no sooner had this hypothetically free person been invented than his liberties were circumscribed by the police power of the state. This was done in the name of republican patriotism, accepts Schama, but the constraints were no less oppressive for that. Just as Mirabeau and the Robespierre of 1791 had feared, liberties were held hostage to the authority of the warrior state.

Violence was not an unpleasant aspect of the revolution, nor did it distract from the accomplishments of the revolution, concludes Schama; it was the motor of the revolution. While it would be grotesque to implicate the generation of 1789 in the kind of hideous atrocities that were perpetrated under the Terror, it would be naïve not to recognize that the former made the latter possible. All the headlines in newspapers, revolutionary festivals, painted plates, songs and street theatre, regiments of little boys waving their arms in the air swearing patriotic oaths in piping voices, all the paraphernalia that was designated as the political culture of the revolution, were the products of the same macabre preoccupation with the just massacre and the heroic death.[5] A violent revolution generated and legitimized state violence in the post-revolutionary phase of French politics.

The lesson is clear. Unless those who practice revolutionary politics understand that violence has to be controlled and managed by political visions and imaginaries, we will land up with nothing but violence in our hearts and gore on our hands. This was precisely the argument that Gandhi had made in 1909.

Gandhi's negation of violence

In *Hind Swaraj*, the 1909 classic written on board the ship that carried Gandhi from London to South Africa, the 'reader' suggests to the 'editor' (who lip syncs for Gandhi) that violence might succeed in securing Indian independence. 'We may have to lose a quarter of a million men, more or less, but we shall regain our land. We shall undertake guerrilla warfare, and defeat the English.' Gandhi's response quivers with outrage, '[d]o you not tremble to think of freeing India by assassination?'[6] Gandhi's incensed response to the suggestion that violence may be able to secure freedom not only addressed the interlocutor and prospective readers, but also practitioners and defenders of a cult of violence that had consumed Indians both in India and in London at the turn of the twentieth century.[7]

He set out to expose the major and the little vanities of political violence. The task was difficult. Though violence was no solution to the problems posed by colonialism, undeniably it *was* the injustice and the violence of the colonial state that had triggered off this cult. In the period following the 1857 revolt, the colonial government set out to implement a policy of vengeance. Rage and resentment at the arrogance, the contempt and the high-handedness of colonial policies built up, accumulated and spilled over into public spaces. Colonial practices had been stripped bare of rhetorical frills and flourishes and revealed for what they were, starkly brutal and essentially dehumanizing. Brought up as they were amidst chilling tales of colonial brutality, educated and often unemployed youth advocated that dishonour could be wiped out, and a sense of self restored to the community, if only they were to pick up the 'gun' and train the barrel at the colonial power. Armed with the conviction that violence by the colonized was the only response to colonial violence, a number of organizations dedicated to the advocacy of this particular form of politics sprang up in the country, particularly in Bengal, Maharashtra, Punjab and the United Provinces. A number of forums were established to provide martial training to young people bent on avenging colonial violence. The partition of Bengal in 1905 set off a chain of reactions from the split of the Congress into the moderates and the extremists, to the upgrading of violence as the currency of politics.

This was the political context in which Gandhi set out to examine violence. The specific trigger for these reflections was the murder of a

British officer Sir Curzon Wylie by a young Indian in London. Hailing from a propertied and an influential Hindu family living in Amritsar, Punjab, Madan Lal Dhingra, as a student in London, came under the influence of V.D. Savarkar. Savarkar at that period of his life tended to lionize and exalt violence.[8] On 10 May 1909, India House radicals organized an annual celebration to honour the martyrs of the 1857 revolt against British colonialism. Speeches brimming over with angst and vengeance peppered the occasion, and charged denunciations of colonial brutality stimulated, or so it appears, this young Indian student to take a life. This was his personal gesture of protest against the hounding of Indian patriots in India.

News of the assassination reached Gandhi who was at that time sailing to London as part of a deputation from Transvaal South Africa. Gandhi was acquainted with Curzon Wylie, but grief at the death of an acquaintance was outstripped by dismay. Violence, he had come to believe by 1909, was not only utterly futile, it was corrupt, corrupting and sterile. Nothing good came out of violence but violence, nothing ever could. This deep conviction had shaped his choice of political strategies – satyagraha, or the pursuit of the truth – against the racist regime in South Africa.

Gandhi's negation of violence was born out of his familiarity with militant revolutionaries in India and with London-based Indians. While in London, Gandhi made it a point to connect with the revolutionaries, attend their meetings and hold extensive discussions on various issues. Their one-sided dedication to the cult of violence appalled him. Despair motivated him to intellectually and politically address political violence. Gandhi consequently embarked on the project of theorizing the nature and the impact of violence, of showing why violence was counterproductive and unproductive as a weapon and of indicating how it could be negated. *Hind Swaraj* was, as he remarked later, his 'answer to the Indian School of violence, and its prototype in South Africa'. 'I', continued Gandhi, 'came in contact with every known Indian anarchist in London. Their bravery impressed me, but I feel that their zeal was misguided. I felt that violence was no remedy for India's ills, and that her civilization required the use of a different and higher weapon for self-protection.'[9]

Gandhi's arguments against violence rested on the belief that this mode of politics is neither pragmatic nor productive. The violence of colonialism is likely to precipitate violence as resistance, but as history shows, the second category simply does not work. In 1920, Gandhi at a public meeting in Calcutta asked the audience to ponder on the history of British rule in India. Did not history, he demanded, demonstrate that Indians have never been able to either resist or counter violence with violence? 'Whilst therefore I say that rather have the yoke of a Government that has so emasculated us, I would welcome violence, I would urge with all the emphasis that I can command that India would never be able to regain her own by methods of violence.'[10] To use violence against a state that possesses superior military technology is to commit political hara-kiri.

Gandhi recognized the enduring and the emasculating power of colonial violence. He appreciated the attraction that violence holds for a people frustrated and exhausted by the depredations of colonialism. But he believed that it was possible to negate violence. If only we knew, Gandhi seemed to suggest, what violence is about we would willingly forswear it. He warned us that the power of violence over human beings must not be underrated. It is best compared to a drug. 'In my view', wrote Gandhi, 'Dhingra was innocent. The murder was committed in a state of intoxication. It is not merely wine or bhang that makes one drunk; a mad idea can do so. That was the case with Dhingra.'[11] He was correct in his reading: Dhingra had reportedly consumed bhang (opium) on the morning he set out to commit an act of political bravado.

The power of violence consumes those who wield it and those who witness it. Therefore, even if independence is won through these means, Gandhi seemed to suggest, people will remain caught in the vice-like grip of this brand of politics. It is simply not possible for them to lay aside violence, as if it were a handy tool employed to hammer a nail into a wall. Even if India could be freed at the cost of torn feet and bloodied hands, her people would never be able to realize what is rightfully theirs or come into 'their own'.

When violence becomes the architect of history, Gandhi suggested, it can only replace one sort of oppression with another sort of oppression. Nothing is transformed if violence is used to craft historical transitions from colonialism to freedom. 'Those who will rise to power by murder will certainly not make the nation happy. Those who believe that India has gained by Dhingra's act and other similar acts in India make a serious mistake. Dhingra was a patriot, but his love was blind. He gave his body in a wrong way; its ultimate result can only be mischievous.'[12]

In sum, Gandhi tells us that negative liberty in the sense of freedom from British colonialism would not serve the purpose of liberation. What is the advantage of acquiring freedom from one set of rulers if another set of rulers replaces them? What is the point, he asked, of acquiring freedom unless people understand freedom in the deeper sense as swaraj or as self-rule.

The concept of swaraj was defined by Gandhi in a number of different ways on different occasions. In 1924, he wrote, 'Swaraj for me means freedom for the meanest of our countrymen ... I am not interested in freeing India merely from the English yoke. I am bent upon freeing India from any yoke whatsoever. I have no desire to exchange King Log for King Stork.'[13] Freedom for him could only be meaningful when the poorest Indian could be freed from want and misery.

Therefore, the enervating effect of violence on popular energies had to be neutralized, and people brought to realization that the attainment of swaraj requires an enormous amount of hard work, courage, commitment, steadfastness and above all a system of public ethics. It is only then that millions could be motivated to struggle together for freedom and reinvent both themselves and society.

Gandhi's notion of violence was theorized inadequately and dwelt upon only as an introduction to the politics of non-violence. It is however remarkable how Gandhi's political perspective on violence as a means to liberation approximated Marxist visions. For Marxists, participation in a common struggle establishes a reciprocal relationship, between collective action and individual sensibilities. Struggle educates, motivates and transforms. No person, once he or she has been radicalized, can ever be the same. And no society, once it has been radicalized, can ever be the same. Gandhi's rejection of irresponsible acts of violence as a catalyst for change was based on a similar logic. Much like the Marxist vanguard, the small body of men and women who had prepared themselves for satyagraha through rigorous training, who intended to challenge all manners of wrong and who were prepared to face the consequences would awaken public opinion. The satyagrahi or those who held steadfastly to the truth, 'must first mobilise public opinion against the evil which he was out to eradicate by means of a wide and intensive agitation … the success of the satyagrahi's efforts must necessarily depend not merely on the appeal to his own conscience *but even more on the awakening of the slumbering conscience of a large number of people*'.[14]

Gandhi's language and imaginaries are of course radically different from those of the Marxists or Maoists. He spoke more of satyagraha as a way of realizing our inner selves that are indispensably ethical and of realizing our connectedness to other people. His satyagrahi does not use violence to overthrow the system. He or she seeks to convert the unjust to justice and to awareness of injustice. Marxist theories of revolution involve standing a system on its head and expunging it of every remnant of injustice or inequality. Gandhi advocated that politics should be embedded in a system of public ethics; it is only then that the rulers come to realize the enormity of injustice and the need for justice. This was his answer to revolutionary militants who worshipped at the altar of violence, and who were completely uninterested in politicizing and mobilizing people in the cause of freedom, making them aware of the possibilities offered by politics, and in building up a mass movement.

The realization of swaraj demands hard work, attention to detail, vast organizing ability and an awakening of national consciousness among the masses. 'It will not spring like the magician's mango. It will grow almost unperceived like the banyan tree. A bloody revolution will never perform the trick. Haste here is most certainly waste.'[15] Without transforming popular consciousness, violence seeks to imprint the body politic. In the process, this mode of politics reduces people to onlookers instead of participants. Conversely, violence becomes a spectator sport.

Proposition III: Democracy and justice

Arguably, there is no essential connection between democracy and justice. A democratic society is not automatically a just society. Most democracies are imperfectly just and therefore inadequately democratic. Justice has to be wrenched out of the greedy hands of individuals and groups who monopolize political, economic, social and cultural power and resources, through struggles that invoke democratic justice. These struggles can range from collective action in civil society to campaigns to revolutionary violence in regions marked by triple injustice. The inspiration for these struggles is the norm of democratic justice; that no one will be denied an equal share in the benefits of society and no one will be forced to shoulder burdens in excess of what others carry. This norm of justice is a broad norm; it can be adjusted for the specific needs of society, for example women, minorities and groups who have been historically disadvantaged, but on balance, it reflects and codifies the basic presupposition of democracy, equality.

Proposition IV: Democracy and revolutionary politics

To address the question asked in the first chapter on the relation between democracy and violence, we can now reiterate that democracy and revolutionary violence occupy the same political space. This metaphorical space has been rendered vacant because democracy has waylaid its own presupposition: that of democratic justice. When institutions of the democratic state foster injustice, when people's interests are betrayed and when the people who are subjected to injustice are faceless both for the state and for civil society, the space that should have been filled in with democratic contestation, social movements, campaigns, protest petitions, marches, demonstrations and strikes becomes vacant. Into this space step in the revolutionaries armed with a vision of a new society that will be free of oppression, exploitation and injustice.

It is then democracy and revolutionary violence occupy the same space. Even if revolutionary violence is riddled with contradictions between theory and practice, it mounts a powerful challenge to violations of democratic justice and to an unfulfilled democratic agenda. In such cases, it is the responsibility of democratic governments to neutralize the challenge and deliver justice to people whose backs have been broken under the burden of triple injustice. Paradoxically, revolutionary politics proves successful in democracies, when it is rendered irrelevant by the institutionalization of justice. The defeat of the revolutionary agenda signifies the success of democracy. The victory of revolutionary politics signifies the defeat of democracy. I am not suggesting that the institutionalization of justice will make violence go away. Violence, we have learnt, is part of the human condition. The political trick is to make it stay on the margins and prevent it from occupying the space of democratic politics. And this can be done, for revolutionary wars are not a law and order problem; these are political wars and have to be dealt with politically. The political negotiation of violence demands innovation, creativity and imagination, but it can be done. Otherwise, violence revolutionary or otherwise will continue to occupy the same space as democracy. And, society will continue to pay heavy costs for the waylaying of democratic justice.

Notes

Introduction

1   Neera Chandhoke, 2011, 'Civil Society in India' in *The Oxford Handbook of Civil Society*, edited by Michael Edwards, Oxford, Oxford University Press, pp. 171–182.

2   In an earlier work I have argued against easy acceptance of secession, because secessions have seldom managed to resolve problems of minorities in the new state. Neera Chandhoke, 2012, *Contested Secessions*, New Delhi, Oxford University Press.

3   'Afghanistan's Insurgency after the Transition' 2014, International Crisis Group, www.crisisgroup.org/en/regions/asia/southAsia/Afghanistan, 12 May, accessed on 16 June 2014.

4   Praveen Swami, 2014, 'War in Iraq hurts every home in India' *The Hindu*, 18 June, p. 10.

5   *Times of India*, 'UN: At 50m, global refugee numbers highest since WWII', 21 June 2014, p. 23.

6   Among some of these works are those of Vittorio Buffachi, 2006, *Violence and Social Justice*, Houndsmill, Basingstoke, Palgrave, Macmillan; Virginia Held, *How Terrorism Is Wrong: Morality and Political Violence*, Oxford, Oxford University Press; C.A.J. Coady, 2007, *Morality and Political Violence*, Cambridge, Cambridge University Press; John Schwarzmantel, 2011, *Democracy and Political Violence*, Edinburg, Edinburgh University Press; Seusmas Miller, 2009, *Terrorism and Counter-Terrorism: Ethics and Liberal Democracy*, Cambridge, Blackwell; R.G. Frey and Christopher W. Morris editors, 1991, *Violence, Terrorism and Justice*, Cambridge, Cambridge University Press.

7   Paul Collier and Anke Hoeffler, 2009, 'Beyond Greed and Grievance: Feasibility and Civil War' *Oxford Economic Papers*, vol 61, no 1, pp. 1–27; James Fearon and David Laitin, 2003, 'Ethnicity, Insurgency

and Civil War' *American Political Science Review*, vol 97, no 1, pp. 75–90. In the case of India, Miklian and Carney argue that the geographical correspondence between mining areas and the region in which Maoists dominate is too stark to be missed. The mines for the authors are the cash registers for the Maoist war chests; they have tapped into these revenues to pay their cadres and buy arms and ammunition; Jason Miklian and Scott Carney (2010) 'Fire in the Hole: How India's Economic Rise Turned an Obscure Communist Revolt into a Raging Resource War' *Foreign Policy*, September/October, no 181, pp. 104–112.

8   John Dunn, 1990, *Interpreting Political Responsibility*, Cambridge, Polity Press, p. 193.

9   Bruno Coppieters, 2003, 'Introduction' in *Contextualizing Secession: Normative Studies in Comparative Perspective*, edited by Bruno Coppieters and Richard Sakwa, Oxford, Oxford University Press, pp. 1–21, pp. 7–8.

10   Daniel McDermott, 2008, 'Analytical Political Philosophy' in *Political Theory: Methods and Approaches*, edited by David Leopold and Marc Stears, Oxford, Oxford University Press, pp. 11–28, p. 11.

11   Plato, 1952, 'Apology' in *The Dialogues of Plato*, translated by Benjamin Jowett, Great Books of the Western World, edited by Robert. M. Hutchins, vol 7, Encyclopedia Brittanica, INC, Chicago, William Benton, pp. 200–212, pp. 202 and 203.

12   M.K. Gandhi, 1991, 'The Vow of Truth' in *The Essential Writings of Mahatma Gandhi*, edited by Raghavan Iyer, New Delhi, Oxford University Press, pp. 223–226, pp. 223–224.

13   Jane Austen, 1813–1972, *Pride and Prejudice*, edited and introduced by Tony Tanner, Harmondsworth, Penguin, p. 236.

14   William Shakespeare, 1952, 'Hamlet' in *The Plays and Sonnets of William Shakespeare*, edited by William G. Clarke and William A. Wright, vol 2, *Great Books of the Western World*, edited by Robert Maynard Hutchins, vol 27, Chicago, William Benton, pp. 29–72, Act 1, scene V, pp. 38.

15   Neera Chandhoke, 2014, 'Negating Violence: The Gandhi Way' in *Between Ethics and Politics: Gandhi Today*, edited by Eva Pfostl, New Delhi, Routledge, pp. 72–97.

Chapter 1

1   William Shakespeare, 1952, *Macbeth*, in *The Plays and Sonnets of William Shakespeare*, vol 2, Great Books of the Western World, edited by Robert Maynard Hutchins, pp. 284–310, in p. 303, Act 4, Scene 3, Chicago, William Benton.

2   Agrima Bhasin, 2014, 'Surviving' *The Hindu*, Sunday Magazine, 12 January, p. 1.

3   Neera Chandhoke and Rajesh Kumar, 2014, 'Indian Democracy: Cognitive Maps' in *Indian Democracy*, edited by K.C. Suri, ICSSR Research Surveys and Explorations, vol 2, general editor Achin Vanaik, New Delhi, Oxford University Press, pp. 17–52, p. 19.

4   Elias Canetti, 1984, *Crowds and Power*, New York, Farrar, Strauss and Giroux, p. 19.

5   Neera Chandhoke, 2012, *Contested Secessions*, New Delhi, Oxford University Press.

6   Barrington Moore Jr, 1966, *Social Origins of Dictatorship and Democracy: Lord and Peasant in the Making of the Modern World*, London, Penguin Books.

7   Moore, *Social Origins of Dictatorship and Democracy*, particularly pp. 413–483.

8   Jason Miklian, 2012, 'The Purification Hunt: The Salwa Judum Counterinsurgency in Chattisgarh India' in *Windows into a Revolution: Ethnographies of Maoism in India and Nepal*, edited by Alpha Shah and Judith Pettigrew, New Delhi, Social Science Press, and New Delhi, Orient BlackSwan, pp. 282–308, p. 293.

9   Miklian, 'The Purification Hunt', p. 302.

10 Miklian, 'The Purification Hunt', p. 297.

11 http://www.supremecourtofindia.nic.in/outtoday/wc25007.pdf, p. 54, accessed on 12 May 2014.

12 M.K. Gandhi, 1965, 'The Doctrine of the Sword', 11 August 1920, *Collected Works of Mahatma Gandhi*, vol XVIII, New Delhi, Government of India, Publications Division, pp. 131–134, p. 132.

13 M.K. Gandhi, 1969, 'Is This Humanity?-IV', 31 October and 4 November 1926, *CWMG*, vol XXXI, pp. 544–547, p. 544.

14 M.K. Gandhi, 1967 'Force or Restraint', 13 July 1924, *CWMG*, vol XXIV, pp. 379–380, p. 379.

Chapter 2

1   Hannah Arendt, 1970, *On Violence*, London, Allen Lane and Penguin, pp. 43–56.

2   Johann Galtung, 1969, 'Violence, Peace and Peace Research' *Journal of Peace Research*, vol 6, no 3, pp. 167–191.

3   C.A.J. Coady, 1999, 'The Idea of Violence' in *Violence and Its Alternatives: An Interdisciplinary Reader*, edited by Manfred B. Steger and Nancy S. Lind, Houndsmill, Macmillan, pp. 23–38.

4   Akhil Gupta, 2012, *Red Tape: Bureaucracy, Structural Violence, and Poverty in India*, Durham, Duke University Press.

5   Akhil Gupta, 2012, *Red Tape: Bureaucracy, Structural Violence, and Poverty in India*, Durham, Duke University Press, p. 21.

6   Vittorio Buffachi, 2006, *Violence and Social Justice*, Houndsmill, Basingstoke, Palgrave, Macmillan, p. 143.

Chapter 3

1   Manoranjan Mohanty, 2006, 'Challenges of Revolutionary Violence: The Naxalite Movement in Perspective' *Economic and Political Weekly*, Special issue on Maoist Movement in India, vol XLI, no 29, 22–28 July, pp. 3163–3168, p. 3163.

2   Sumanta Bannerjee, 2006, 'Beyond Naxalbari' *Economic and Political Weekly*, vol XLI, no 29, 22–28 July 2006, pp. 3159–3192, p. 3159.

3   *India Human Development Report 2011 Towards Social Inclusion*, Planning Commission, Government of India and Institute of Applied Manpower Research, New Delhi, Oxford University Press, p. 3, p. 17, p. 18. An update to the report was released by the Institute in 2014, Aarti Dhar, 2014, 'Human Development indicators are on the upswing in Bimaru States', *The Hindu*, 14 March 2014. The report included Uttarakhand in the category of poorer states and excluded West Bengal.

4   UNDP, 2010, *Human Development Report 'The Real Wealth of Nations: Pathways to Human Development'*, p. 99, http://hdr.undp.org, accessed on 31 March 2011.

5   *The Caravan, A Journal of Politics and Culture*, http://www. caravanmagazine.in, accessed on 15 August 2013.

6   Ministry of Rural Development, Government of India, 2009, *Report of Sub-Group IV of Committee on State Agrarian Relations and Unfinished Tasks of Land Reform*, vol 1, http://dolr.nic.in/agrarian_committee.htm, accessed on 20 March 2012, chapter 4.

7   Government of India, 2008, *Development Challenges in Extremist Affected Areas: Report of an Expert Group to Planning Commission*, www. planningcommission.gov.in/reports/publications/rep_dce.pdf, accessed on 11 November 2012, p. 8.

8   Government of India, 2008, *Development Challenges in Extremist Affected Areas*, p. 7.

9   According to D'Mello, the main players are Arcelor Mittal, Essar Group, Vedanta Resources, Tata Steel, Posco, Rio Tinto, BHP Billiton, and Sajjan Jindal group. Bernard D'Mello, 2010, 'Spring Thunder Anew, Neo-Robber Baron Capitalism vs "New Democracy" in India', http://monthlyreview.org/commentary/spring-thunder-anew, accessed on 19 March 2012, p. 17.

10 *Committee on State Agrarian Relations and Unfinished Tasks of Land Reform*, vol 1, conclusion to chapter IV, http://www.rd.ap.gov.in/ IKPLand/MRD-committee-report-V-01Mar_09.pdf.

Chapter 4

1   Amreeta Syam, 1992, 'Kurukshetra' in *Vyasa's Mahabharat: Creative Insights*, edited by P. Lal, Calcutta, A Writers Workshop Publication, pp. 13–17.

2   Niccolo Machiavelli, 1998, *The Prince*, edited with an introduction and notes by Peter Bondanella, translated by Peter Bondanella and Mark Musa, Oxford, Oxford University Press, p. 82.

3   Plato, 1984, 'Crito [Or, On What Is to Be Done]' in *Plato and Aritophanes: Four Texts on Socrates*, translated and with notes by Thomas G. West and Grace S. West, introduction by Thomas G. West, Ithaca, Cornell University Press, pp. 99–114, pp. 109–111.

4   I am obliged to Achin Vanaik for pointing this out to me.

5   Sophocles, 1960, 'Antigone' in *Great Books of the Western World*, edited
     by Robert Maynard Hutchins, Chicago, William Benton Publishers,
     pp. 131–142, p. 135.
6   The case of Darshan Singh versus the State of Punjab and another. The
     Court ruled on 15 January 2012, http://www.vakilno1.com, accessed on
     1 July 2012, para 24.
7   *The Mahabharata of Krishna-Dwaipayana Vyasa*, translated by Kisari
     Mohan Ganguly, vol VIII, Santi Parva, Part I, Delhi, Munshiram
     Manoharlal Publishers Pvt. Ltd, pp. 1–2.
8   *The Mahabharata of Krishna-Dwaipayana Vyasa*, Section LVI, p. 113
9   *The Mahabharata of Krishna-Dwaipayana Vyasa*, p. 122.
10   *The Mahabharata of Krishna-Dwaipayana Vyasa*, Section LXVII, p. 146.
11   *The Mahabharata of Krishna-Dwaipayana Vyasa*, p. 146.
12   Chaturvedi Badrinath, 2006, *The Mahabharata: An Inquiry into the
     Human Condition*, Hyderabad, Orient Longmans, p. 418.
13   Chaturvedi Badrinath, *The Mahabharata*, pp. 419–420.
14   *The Mahabharata of Krishna-Dwaipayana Vyasa*, Section LVI, p. 116.
15   *The Mahabharata of Krishna-Dwaipayana Vyasa*, Section XCI, pp.
     199–200.
16   John Locke, 1988, 'The Second Treatise of Government: An Essay
     Concerning the True Original, Extent and End of Civil Government'
     in *Two Treatises of Government*, edited and introduced by Peter Laslett,
     Cambridge, Cambridge University Press, p. 415.
17   Thomas Hobbes, 1988, *The Leviathan*, Amherst, Prometheus Books.

Chapter 5

1   Sumanta Bannerjee, 2012, 'Reflections of a One-Time Maoist Activist' in
     More than Maoism: Politics, Policies and Insurgencies in South Asia, edited
     by Robin Jeffrey, Ronojoy Sen and Pratima Singh, New Delhi, Manohar,
     pp. 47–68, p. 54.
2   Georg Kunnath, 2012, 'Smouldering Dalit Fires in Bihar' in *Window
     into a Revolution: Ethnographies of Maoism in India and Nepal*, edited by
     Alpha Shah and Judith Pettigrew, New Delhi, Social Science Press and
     Orient Blackswan, pp. 89–112.

3   Frantz Fanon, 1985 edn, *The Wretched of the Earth*, translated by
    Constance Farrington, Middlesex, Penguin Books.

4   Fanon, *The Wretched of the Earth*, p. 74.

5   Fanon, *The Wretched of the Earth*, p. 74.

6   Jean Paul Sartre, Preface to Frantz Fanon, *The Wretched of the Earth*,
    pp. 7–26, p. 19.

7   Fanon, *The Wretched of the Earth*, p. 111.

8   Fanon, *The Wretched of the Earth*, pp. 112–113.

9   Fanon, *The Wretched of the Earth*, p. 114.

10 Fanon, *The Wretched of the Earth*, p. 115.

11 Fanon, *The Wretched of the Earth*, p. 165.

12 Fanon, *The Wretched of the Earth*, p. 118, italics added.

13 Leo Tolstoy, 1961, *War and Peace*, translated from Russian by Constance
    Garnet, London, Heinemann, p. 977, p. 978, p. 1019, p. 1020.

14 Che Guevara, 1961, *Guerrilla Warfare*, New York, Monthly Review Press,
    p. 17.

15 Guevara, *Guerrilla Warfare*, p. 17.

16 Guevara, *Guerrilla Warfare*, p. 15.

17 Gerard Chaliand, 1977, *Revolution in the Third World: Myths and
    Prospects*, Sussex, Harvester Press, p. 44, p. 47.

18 Henry Bienen, 1977, 'State and Revolution: The Work of Amilcar Cabral'
    Journal of Modern African Studies, vol 15, no 4, pp. 555–568.

19 Mao Tse-tung, 'What is GuerrillaWarfare?', www.marxists.org.org/
    reference/archive/mao/works/1937/guerrilla-warfare/ch01.htm, accessed
    on 11 March 2013.

20 Antonio Gramsci, 1996, *Selections from the Prison Notebooks of Antonio
    Gramsci*, edited and translated by Quintin Hoare and Geoffrey Nowell
    Smith, Hyderabad, Orient Longmans, p. 322.

21 Alpha Shah, 2012, 'Markets of Protection. The "Terrorist" Maoist
    Movement and the State in Jharkand India' in *Window into a
    Revolution: Ethnographies of Maoism in India and Nepal*, edited by
    Alpha Shah and Judith Pettigrew, New Delhi, Social Science Press and
    Orient Blackswan.

22 Bela Bhatia, 2006, 'On Armed Resistance' *Economic and Political Weekly*,
    Special issue on Maoist Movement in India, vol XLI, no 29, 22–28 July,
    pp. 3179–3182, pp. 3181–3182.

23 Bernard D'Mello, 2010, 'Spring Thunder Anew, Neo-Robber Baron Capitalism vs "New Democracy" in India', 21 March 2010, http:// monthlyreview.org/commentary/spring-thunder-anew, accessed on 19 March 2012.

24 Bannerjee, 'Beyond Naxalbari', pp. 3159–3163, p. 3159.

25 Bernard D'Mello, 2010, 'Spring Thunder Anew, Neo-Robber Baron Capitalism vs "New Democracy" in India', 21 March 2010, http:// monthlyreview.org/commentary/spring-thunder-anew, accessed on 19 March 2012, p. 17.

26 Nirmalangshu Mukherjee, 2010, 'Arms Over the People: What Have the Maoists Achieved in Dandakaranya?' *Economic and Political Weekly*, vol XLV, no 25, 19 June, pp. 16–20, p. 17.

27 Nandini Sundar, 2006, 'Bastar, Maoism and Salwa Judum' *Economic and Political Weekly*, Special issue on Maoist Movement in India, vol XLI, no 29, 22–28 July, pp. 3187–3192, pp. 3189–3190.

28 Sundar, 'Bastar, Maoism and Salwa Judum', p. 18.

29 John Harriss, 2012, 'What Is Going on in India's "Red Corridor"? Questions About India's Maoist Insurgency' in *More Than Maoism: Politics, Policies and Insurgencies in South Asia*, edited by Robin Jeffrey, Ronojoy Sen and Pratima Singh, New Delhi, Manohar, pp. 25–46, pp. 40–41.

30 Tilak D. Gupta, 2006, 'Maoism in India: Ideology, Programme and Armed Struggle' *Economic and Political Weekly*, Special issue on Maoist Movement in India, vol XLI, no 29, 22–28 July, pp. 3172–3176, pp. 3172–3173.

31 Bannerjee, 'Reflections of a One-Time Maoist Activist', pp. 47–68, pp. 59–60.

Conclusion

1 Patrick Chabal, 1983, *Amilcar Cabral: Revolutionary Leadership and People's War*, Cambridge, Cambridge University Press, p. 172.

2 Chalmers Johnson, 1962, *Peasant Nationalism and Communist Power*, Stanford, Stanford University Press, p. ix.

3 Bannerjee, 'Reflections of a One-Time Maoist Activist', pp. 47–68, pp. 59–60.

4   There are other ways of transforming politics, social movements for instance, but here the argument is in the context of revolutionary violence.

5   Simon Schama, 1989, *Citizens: A Chronicle of the French Revolution*, London, Penguin, pp. 858–860.

6   M.K. Gandhi, 2006, *Hind Swaraj or Indian Home Rule*, Ahmedabad, Navjivan Trust, p. 60.

7   The 1909 edition of *Hind Swaraj* is politically significant because it addressed the political context in India: revolutionary terrorism and the 1907 split in the Indian National Congress. Gandhi had to negotiate ardent advocates of violence, as well as the politics of mendicancy that the Congress had become famous for.

8   Savarkar (1883–1966) argued strenuously for a guerrilla war against the colonial government on the same lines as the 1857 uprising, which he termed the First War of Independence. In London, he was a regular visitor to India House set up by Shyamji Krishnaverma that had become a centre of radical politics by Indian students in London. Savarkar's rhetoric reportedly cast a spell on many a young man in London. He certainly influenced Dhingra greatly. In his recollections, *Six Glorious Epochs of Indian History* Savarkar wrote that Dhingra was 'converted to our revolutionary views through my principles and guidance'. Cited in V.N. Dutta, 1978, *Madan Lal Dhingra and the Revolutionary Movement*, New Delhi, Vikas Publishing House, p. 51.

9   M.K. Gandhi, 1966, 'Hind Swaraj or the "Indian Home Rule"', 16 January 1921, *Collected Works of Mahatma Gandhi, New Delhi, Government of India, Publications Division*, vol XIX, pp. 277–278, p. 277.

10 M.K. Gandhi, 1966, 'Speech on Non-Cooperation, Calcutta', 22 December 1920, *Collected Works of Mahatma Gandhi*, vol XIX, pp. 102–107.

11 Cited in V.N. Dutta, p. 72.

12 M.K. Gandhi, *Hind Swaraj*, p. 60.

13 M.K. Gandhi, 1924, 'Untouchability and Swaraj, 12 June 1924, Collected Works of Mahatma Gandhi', vol XXIV, May–August 1924, Publications Division, Government of India, 1967, pp. 226–27, p. 227.

14 Raghavan Iyer, 1973, *The Moral and Political Thought of Mahatma Gandhi*, New Delhi, Oxford University Press, p. 286.

15 M.K. Gandhi, *Young India*, 21 May 1925, p. 178.

Index

Note: The letter 'n' following locators refers to notes.

www.ingramcontent.com/pod-product-compliance
Lightning Source LLC
Chambersburg PA
CBHW062030270326
41929CB00014B/2387